M000198777

1/22/2022

Daniel,

I am excited abou dad's newest book, on spiritual Warfare! This shares how God's word tells us how we can have supernatural protection. This book will also give you more insight into some of my dad's background and how it prepared him to be one of God's soldiers (2 Timothy 2:3).

PERISH

Without

SPIRITUAL WARFARE

I'm really, it also shows a bit about my past. I pray this book, with Gods word, blesses you and your family.

Ephesians 6: 10-18

Psalm 91

God Bless! Steve Lummebi

BOOKS by David F. Winecoff

Forward March
SECRET WEAPON: Men Overcoming Chaos

(These books and other writings and essays
are found at
www.waragoodwarfare.com)

ADVANCE PRAISE

"My husband started reading this book, sparking deep conversation between us. He read it to me every night and it created a closer walk and open conversation about how wonderful God is. It got us closer than ever. Wonderful read!" Holly Farnsworth, Granbury, TX

"With the discipline and diligence of a military man, Winecoff arms you with the power of the Holy Spirit in the battle against worldly evils. Through personal example, he strategically outlines how to keep the Holy Spirit thriving in the mind and body. Good read!" Heidi Quinn, Ellensburg, WA

"...It got me reading the Bible for the first time. It showed me how I could be – not how I thought I was – in my relationship with Jesus. Every veteran should read this book." Al Bragg, Cle Elum, WA

"I was intimidated to start this book because of the topic of 'Spiritual Warfare.' ...Dave, through his personal experiences and God's word, gave me strength without fear to fight my own battles with the help of the Holy Spirit." Wendy Ringen, Ellensburg, Washington

"I am the Mission Pastor at Real Life Ministries in Post Falls, Idaho. It was a blessing and a pleasure to read your book. It contains many, many important truths that are needed and critical in our time and in the current 'world culture.' Your perspective as a soldier was unique and helpful." Dave Campbell, Post Falls, ID

"This remarkable book takes the struggle from the early years which entangled and surrounded us and introduces scripture and devotion to walk us through war times of our past and carries us into our present-day battle. You may ask, 'What is Spiritual Warfare, and why it is important?' It is often a term used among Christians. In scripture, Paul speaks of this battle in Ephesians 6:11-12, [11]Put on the full armor of God, so that you can take your stand against the devil's schemes. [12]For our struggle is not against flesh and blood, but against the rulers, against the authorities, against the powers of this dark world, and the spiritual forces of evil in the heavenly realms of the *Perish Without Spiritual Warfare.*" Patricia (Pat) Cort, Kittitas, WA

PERISH

Without

SPIRITUAL WARFARE

By

David F. Winecoff

Lt Colonel USMC – Retired

(SPIRITUAL WARFARE:
The Art of Declaring
God's Word in defense of someone you
love or something of value)

Winecoff

Dave

Psalm 50:15

Reecer Creek Publishing
Ellensburg, Washington

Dedication

To the family and friends of Medal of Honor recipient William D. Morgan, a beloved member of Hotel Company, 2d Battalion, 9th Marines, 3d Marine Division. Cpl. Morgan was honored for conspicuous gallantry and intrepidity at the risk of his life above and beyond the call of duty while serving as a squad leader in Quang Tri Province, Republic of Vietnam, on 25 February 1969. His heroic and determined actions saved the lives of two fellow marines and were instrumental in the subsequent defeat of the enemy. He gallantly gave his life in upholding the highest traditions of the Marine Corps.

Foreword

I am honored to have been asked by my father to write the foreword for his new book on spiritual warfare. My father is a man of great faith and integrity. He deeply loves God, our family, and our nation.

So, why is this book on spiritual warfare so important? Many say we are in the last days as described in 2 Timothy 3:1-5. This book provides a unique perspective on spiritual warfare from a modern-day warrior and watchman who has spent decades studying the word of God. Jeremiah 6:17 says, "Also I sent watchmen over you, saying, Hearken to the sound of the trumpet. But they said, "We will not hearken." The question is, who is willing to listen to one of our modern-day "watchmen?"

Steven D. Winecoff, Former Captain
2d Battalion, 2d Marines
Post Falls, Idaho

Preface

In 1968, a difficult time in my life, before I had become spiritually aware enough to write this book, I left my family to return to South Vietnam for a 3d combat tour. When I joined my rifle company, I was shocked by the profane language in use. Many were not expressing themselves without the use of vulgarity in almost every sentence. This often-rough language has severe consequences if one suddenly finds himself standing in front of his maker. Protests were seriously increasing back home. This rough language was probably in direct proportion to the increase in anti-war activities in the States! Over two nights while on radio watch, I penned an impassioned article to send off to the Marine Corps Gazette Magazine for publication. I did this under a poncho with a flashlight and passed it to the Company Gunny to share my feelings with the men about such language. After making the rounds, he sent it to the rear to be mailed off. The remainder of the time I commanded that rifle company, nine months, I heard very little profanity within earshot. Remarkable how men can turn such language off when motivated to do so. The death angel stalks us all. What comes out of our mouths should be of far greater concern than it often is because death can be sudden.

Recently I searched to see if I could find that article on the internet: I found it under the title: *"English not Anglo-Saxon with my name."* Upon my return from overseas and following some schooling at Fort Benning, Georgia, I was assigned to the Basic School at Quantico, Virginia, from 1970-73 as a tactic's instructor. I was assigned to the

Patrolling Department. There I met Lieutenant Oli North. It was a privilege to be part of this dynamic instruction team.

For eighteen months, I helped teach new officers how to patrol, raid, ambush, and otherwise create mischief in the enemy-held territory, mostly at night. Oli was clearly the student's favorite instructor. They nicknamed him *"True North."* We did a lot of compass work. Later I was reassigned to the Squad Tactics section for a year and then given a student company of 240 students to take through the six-month training course. Years later, following retirement from military service, I involved myself in politics. For eight years, I was a city councilman in Mill Creek, Washington north of Seattle. Two years into that experience, I ran to become a Washington State legislator. Oli had gained the nation's attention during the televised Iran Contra hearings and later became a television personality. He came through Seattle on a speaking tour. I sought him out to catch up. When he heard I was running for a position as a republican state legislator, he wrote me a very complimentary endorsement. I don't know whether it was his endorsement in such a liberal arena or the very expensive brochure my opponent put out in the last week before the vote that I couldn't match financially: but I lost my lead and the race. I did gain the most votes of the seven of us running against liberal incumbents that year while spending the least amount of money. A small satisfaction. It taught me how hard it is as a conservative in a liberal state to beat an incumbent. I could not run the following term because of a family problem, but one of my supporters maintained our campaign momentum and defeated him the next time around.

Oli's endorsement meant a lot to me. It was not easy keeping quiet in the Greater Seattle area as a conservative. Many rational opinions cannot be shared with closed minds. You indeed find yourself isolated as a conservative in such an environment. And it has only gotten worse. Seattle has earned its antiwar reputation. As with war, I learned politics can be a nasty, rough, and tumble business. Running for public office three times certainly challenged me. But I do not believe Christians should shy away from such endeavors. Though there is a personal cost, we cannot give these important arenas over to those who see life so differently.

So, what qualifies me to write about how war and life are connected to biblical prophecy and spiritual warfare? At 81, I have been a believer almost longer than I can remember. I love to read. I have been studying the Bible for the last 42 years. I have been a student of warfare even longer. In 1979, I was still on active duty, and it was five years after our official withdrawal from Vietnam. I was stationed in Washington State and read the Everett Herald Newspaper's weekend edition with some morning coffee. There was a four-page section on the Vietnam War and its aftermath. One sentence greatly impacted my spirit. You might say I had a paradigm shift in my understanding.

"Since the recent end of the war in Vietnam three times as many veterans had committed suicide as those killed in combat, and in the last year tallied: 91% of the single-car fatalities were military veterans." At that moment, I suddenly realized a hidden war I had failed to notice was raging: killing, maiming, and destroying men, women, and children across the planet! While I prepared for the next likely U.S. engagement overseas, a much larger and more deadly war was ongoing that I had failed to notice. At that moment, I decided to retire from military service to focus on this mostly unnoticed war. I thought with retirement, I would have more freedom as a working civilian to become engaged as a different kind of warfighter: a more spiritual one in a heavenly army. Few believers understand the nature of this kind of warfare. I certainly had not. How to survive at the individual level and how to fight back using spiritual tools God has given us, I had little knowledge of such skills! I had no idea what my studies would uncover at the time of my decision.

When you read this book, I hope this different vantage point I bring will help you see the importance of this fight through new eyes. The Bible in Psalms and elsewhere exhorts fathers to pass on to their children overcoming faith to sustain them amid their fiery trials. It is best to equip children at an early age to fight spiritually. This book is about how to overcome in the presence of the enemy. **(Psalm 23:5)** The world should be a far safer place for women and children than it is. It's my sad observation that few parents or adults have any deep understanding of the depth of evil going on or the supernatural help available to counter this evil. Satan is presently the god of this world. He is clever. His influence remains mostly hidden. He is adept at camouflaging his presence. Because of his deceptive ways, there is an allusion of peace and safety in many minds. But it is mostly just an illusion. Satan has more influence and control than most ever become aware of. This book is written for my children, grandchildren, great-grandchildren, and those who choose to read and share this work. I am the first in my extended family to live past 80 years. Many stronger, smarter men in my limited field of vision, some close friends have now passed before they had a chance to engage in such a task. Many of these military peers were not, to my knowledge, born again believers. This troubles me. P.T.S.D. and other underlying medical conditions are formidable enemies that further hamper such a personal research undertaking in the final third of one's life span. My wife and I are in the golden years and in excellent health. Neither of us takes any doctor prescribed medicines. Is this just luck, strong genes, a healthy diet, or could it also have something to do with who is looking out for us and the promises of God? I am shocked at the many who are far younger and dependent on drugs. Many are disabled in so many ways. It is certainly not God's best for them. Scripture makes it quite clear in **1 John 3:8** that a war is going on: *"... For this purpose, the Son of God was manifested, that he might destroy the works of the devil."* Brothers and sisters, are those in your intimate community really taking the devil and God's promises seriously. Or do you see what I see many with their guard down? There seems to be a lot of blindness and deception across the land. This book is written to sound the alarm. Much of the world is seriously blinded. **(II Cor. 4:4)**

The real beginning of my spiritual journey followed my wake-up call well into adult life once I seriously picked up the Bible and began to believe what I read. Until then, I was just an every Sunday Christian, seriously deficient in wisdom and knowledge. We must choose to walk out of the blindness that grips so many.

I marvel, as the world has grown darker morally, that I seldom hear spontaneous personal testimonies of God's goodness from pulpits on Sunday mornings or while having coffee with friends. When God shows his power, it is such an exciting thing. Satan works hard to keep us ignorant. He wants to keep us from sharing our spiritual victories with others. Learning about healings, deliverances, provisions, safety, and answered prayers from God himself through his written word and from hearing personal testimonies in Full Gospel Businessmen's Fellowship, International circles during the 70s and 80s were wonderful. Now the world has grown darker as the Bible says it would. ~David F. Winecoff

Acknowledgments

I want to acknowledge and thank my good friend, Kent Davault, who came to me with a title and suggested chapter contents, and suggested I write a book: *"a Marine Colonel looks at Spiritual Warfare."* Kent's life focus is soul winning. He loves to lead worship while singing and playing his guitar or banjo. He knows hundreds of full gospel songs. He covets the gift of prophecy. Very scriptural! A good friend to have. Also this book could not have been published without the generous financial support of Roger Reynolds.

Also, I want to acknowledge another friend, Pat Cort, who formatted this book for me. It was a challenge because she is very busy with VFW and the City of Kittitas projects and a husband, Dennis, also a good friend who keeps her hopping. They have a large family. Also, I want to acknowledge Al Bragg, our VFW Post Commander, who encouraged me to publish this book.

Also, I want to acknowledge my wife, Karen. With love, she encourages and challenges me spiritually as a good wife should. She is a wonderful mother, homemaker, and hostess. Definitely a Proverbs 31 woman; and my best friend. And to our wonderful family.

And finally, to our Heavenly Father for his love and forgiveness; and to Jesus for his sacrifice and great example; and to the Holy Spirit for enabling us to be more and do more than we ever thought possible.

Table of Contents

Opening Challenges

"Cursed is the one who refuses to fight." **Jeremiah 48:10**

"For the weapons of our warfare are not carnal, but mighty through God to the pulling down of strong holds; Casting down imaginations, and every high thing that exalteth itself against the knowledge of God and bringing into captivity every thought to the obedience of Christ." ~2 **Corinthians 10:4**

Prophesied coming Famine of the Word

"Behold, the days come, saith the Lord GOD, that I will send a famine in the land, not a famine of bread, nor a thirst for water, but of hearing the words of the LORD: And they shall wander from sea to sea, and from the north even to the east, they shall run to and fro to seek the word of the LORD, and shall not find it." ~Amos 8:11-12

"...Though these three men were in it; as I live, saith the Lord GOD, they shall deliver neither sons nor daughters; they only shall be delivered, but the land shall be desolate ~Ezekiel 14: 14, 16, 18 and 20

Footnote: It seems these Old Testament prophecies will be fulfilled in the Great Tribulation, which could begin in our generation. The light of Jesus Christ is systematicallybeing put out here in America. And across the world, the light is growing darker at an alarming speed.

xvi

1

AN OVERCOMING FAITH

In these increasingly dangerous times, how to live a God kind of faith is absolutely needed. To live an overcoming life as believers, with all life's challenges, we need divine help. Scripture tells us a lot about this kind of faith. It is the faith Jesus called twice *"great faith."* He saw it in a Roman centurion soldier and also in a non-Jewish woman. That was recorded! Hopefully, he saw it in others too. It is certainly not common in the average community of believers that I have observed in this season of the Co-vid 19 pandemic.

"But without faith, it is impossible to please him: for he that cometh to God must believe that he is and that he is a rewarder of them that diligently seek him." ~**Hebrews 11:6**

In the first part of my life, I was somewhat aware of the spiritual dimensions of life as a young adult. I hoped I pleased God. But was seldom ever completely sure! He was not my main focus as I went about my daily life. I see that plainly looking back. I had a religious upbringing—the Roman Catholic kind of faith. I faithfully attended weekly mass. I practiced what the church taught me. I memorized a half dozen prayers growing up. I prayed them daily. I resisted sinning as best I knew how. I knew the importance of confession and forgiveness and practiced these tenets. I did have a certain *"fear of the Lord."* The Bible is clear: this is the beginning of wisdom. It kept me from some sin that took down others around me. Many that seemed to me to have more promise than I thought I was endowed with!

At the age of 39, I had a startling spiritual experience. This event showed me how little I really knew spiritually. This experience came soon after I decided to read the Bible daily and began doing so. I set a goal of at least ten minutes a night. This decision was made after thinking: How can I call myself a Christian if I am not reading the Bible, which I wasn't up to that point. In fact, I never opened it. It was sadly an adornment on our coffee table.

Certainly, I was exposed to passages of scripture weekly in the mass and daily during Lent, both the Old and New Testaments. For 39 years, I believed that practicing the sacraments of the church were enough. In all that time, I had never opened a Bible on my own or memorized even one verse of scripture. I can't remember ever hearing this was an important thing to do from any priest, nun, or lay leader.

faith not hope

Soon after I began the daily reading of the Bible, I realized that my faith was misdirected. It had been in an institution, the Catholic Church, certainly not, toward the living God! Was there really only one mediator between God and man, Jesus Christ? I thought it was my local Catholic priest. For the first half of my life, I had been praying in hope, not faith. Hope is directed toward the future. Faith is a now thing. Do we want our prayers answered now, or in the future? Is real salvation a new thing or something that will happen in the

2

future? I never was sure as a Roman Catholic where I stood with God.

*"Now, faith is the substance of things hoped for, the evidence of things not seen." ~**Hebrews 11:1***

The God kind of faith sees something spiritually before it materializes into the natural realm. What do I mean? We all need to fully realize who God is and who we are in Christ, Jesus. He is the God who answers a believer's prayers. When we have prayed a prayer that we believe God wants to answer, we can know after praying that He has dispatched an angel in response to our request. If we have read **the Book of Daniel,** we learned that God immediately dispatched an angel when Daniel prayed. But it took that mighty angel 21 days to battle through the realm of the fallen angels (evidence of the spiritual warfare that goes on) to bring Daniel the answer to his prayer. To communicate with God, we have to know ourselves, our God, and the spiritual situation. Real patience awaits God's answer to real prayers.

examine yourself

*"Examine yourselves, whether ye be in the faith: prove your own selves. Know ye, not your own selves, how that Jesus Christ is in you, except ye be reprobates?" ~**II Corinthians 13:5***

All my conscious life, I thought of myself as a Christian. I thought all Christians were believers until I became one. What do I mean? At the age of 39, I had a radical perception change due to a dramatic life-changing encounter with the living God. It so impacted my understanding that I kept silent about it for two years. I never even told my wife at the time! Before that open-eyed vision occurring over 50 minutes, I was under the illusion I knew what I needed to know spiritually to live a decent life. I was not perfect! None of us are! But I thought I was bound for

3

heaven, not hell, and served God as best I could under the circumstances. But mine was a religious approach to God.

*"There is a way which seemeth right unto a man, but the end thereof are the ways of death." ~**Proverbs 14:12***

My first ever vision at the age of 39 showed me how deceived I had been as a believing Christian. Married with children and a professional Marine, I was busy and distracted enough, not even to be aware of my daily need for Bible study. That is what we all need to gain a truly spiritual perspective. It never occurred to me I was deceived. I was mostly happy in my blindness. Things were generally going well for me. Looking back over my life, following my vision experience, I see my focus was off the mark. I mainly was going it alone concerning my responsibilities as a husband, father, and Marine. God was not in my life in the way he desired to be.

Since that impactful night in the early Spring of 1978 on the island of Okinawa at 9 pm in the quiet of my B.O.Q., room at Camp Hansen, while reading my Bible, everything has changed. God communicated with me through a powerful vision. I became aware of the spiritual realm in a way I had never known. My knowledge of my spirituality went from theoretical and academic to very real and personal. The spiritual realm forever replaced the natural realm in its importance for me.

a personal vision

I had been ordered for a year to a combat-ready assignment as the Operations and Training Officer of a 5,000-man infantry regiment, the 4th Marine Regiment, unaccompanied by family. The point of the spear for rapid deployment in the Far East. I was a major. It was an important assignment. I had to say goodbye to my family for a full year. My leaving was hard for us all. My going was to the same regiment my dad was with in China for three years before the Second World War. I was born into this regiment as a baby. Here I was back in it as an adult. Was this a mere coincidence?

Since I would be away for twelve months, I made a list of things I wanted to accomplish after working hours. One of those tasks was to read the New Testament, Psalms, and Proverbs, which I had never done before. At the three-month point, I realized I was making progress on each of the other six tasks I had written down except for the reading of the Bible. So, I pulled the pocket New Testament the Marine Corps had issued me that I had carried during my last Vietnam combat tour out of my duffle bag. Setting it on the nightstand beside my bed, I said aloud to myself: *"Ten minutes a night."* I opened this pocket-sized booklet and began to read **the Book of Matthew**. I remember exactly where the Lord first grabbed my attention. It was:

"I indeed baptize you with water unto   repentance: but he that cometh after me is mightier than I whose shoes I am not worthy to bear: he shall baptize you with the Holy Ghost, and with fire; Whose fan is in his hand, and he will thoroughly purge his floor, and gather his wheat into the garner, but he will burn up the chaff with unquenchable fire." ~*Matthew* **3:11-12**

When I read this passage, I was flooded with a warm feeling that washed over my body. A few days later, I read these same verses in **Luke 3:16.** I got that same sensation all over again. I remember thinking, what is this sensation? I had not experienced it before. I felt God was signaling a spiritual change in my life and to read on. Until these two quickening's of my spirit when I heard scripture, it was nice, but I had heard much of it before, being read at Sunday morning mass weekly throughout my life. When it happened a second time, I read the rest of **Luke**, all of **John** and **Acts** that night; this was the night of the vision. I remember distinctly my excitement when I read **John 3:3 and 6** about being born again. I must have heard these passages before.

But for the first time, they grabbed my attention. I was startled by realizing that religious training and practices were not the same as being born again. Yes, I had received the sacraments of communion, penance, and confirmation, along with instruction on their importance for a religious person. Also, the sacrament of matrimony! Weekly I had taken communion most of my life, and occasionally I went to confession when I was being convicted. I knew things in my head. But my heart had not been impacted like it was being impacted this incredible night. I continued reading. I got to **John 20:22** and read this:

"And when he had said this, he breathed on them, and saith unto them, Receive ye the Holy Ghost:"

the promise of the father

At this, I got excited. I felt something new was happening to me. I read on and into **the Book of Acts**; many verses impacted and excited me that wonderful night. One of the earlier verses in **Luke 24:49** was:

"And behold, I send the promise of my Father upon you: but tarry ye in the city of Jerusalem, until ye be endued with power from on high."

I read through all of chapter one and into chapter two of **Acts** very excited. When I got to **Acts 2:38**, I read this:

"Then Peter said unto them, Repent, and be baptized every one of you in the name of Jesus Christ for the remission of sins, and ye shall receive the gift of the Holy Ghost."

standing up

At this point, I stood to my feet, looked up toward heaven, unconsciously raised my hands in the surrender position, and made a strong declaration, communicating my heart's desire to God: *"I want what you are giving here in this verse, LORD."* Meaning the gift of the Holy Ghost.

6

Instantly the far wall and half the ceiling where my eyes were focused scrolled back. I saw into the spiritual realm. Jesus Christ was alive before me. He seemed to be about 30 feet away, just beyond the edge of my room. He was indeed the Lord of heaven and earth. What I saw was described, I saw later that night, in **Psalms 104: 2-3**

"Who coverest thyself with light as with a garment: who stretchest out the heavens like a curtain: Who layeth the beams of his chambers in the waters: who maketh the clouds his chariot: "

I had looked at the clock just before the vision started: It was 9 pm! When the vision ended, I noticed the clock again, 9:50 pm. For 50 minutes, I had watched Jesus in intercession for his people on earth. Three times as he turned in my direction, he made eye contact, slightly nodding, showing he was aware of my presence. His back was never toward me. He was busy praying for those things that were in his Father's heart. We did not speak. I watched in awe and wonder. I was fully aware of my surroundings in the room, but that was not my focus. What I saw beyond the veil through spiritual eyes was so very real. I saw not just Jesus, but the vast space and stars that were his backdrop.

a distracting thought

I need to tell you what ended the vision, a religious thought: *"I am seeing what the saints of old called the Beatific Vision."* I had read about it as a teenager in a biography about one of the saints. *"I should be on my knees, I thought!"* As I moved to get on my knees, the vision suddenly ended. I was looking again at only my wall and ceiling. But the presence of the Holy Spirit remained strong on me for hours longer. The remainder of that night until the rays of the sun came into the room that following morning, I stayed in the Word of God, wanting more. God communicated with me, taking me to various verses that impacted my spirit. He had answered my holy declaration giving me the promise of the Father. I later learned

Pentecostals call this the Baptism of the Holy Ghost. I had never heard this term during any Roman Catholic religious instruction. It was a foreign term to me. What a fiery, wonderful night like no other. I never got tired all that night or the next day. What a high!

the next morning

Two calls quickly came the next morning—both calls telling me the good news. First, my former wife's call! Our empty house in Virginia had sold for a reasonable price with a quick closing. For us, a miracle! It had been on the market for nine months through the winter. We had moved the family to Washington State and bought a new home in Mill Creek near both sets of parents. While I was overseas, we had been paying double mortgage payments. We thought our last home would have sold quickly. The stress was difficult. We were within one month of bankruptcy. Not suitable for one's health, career, family, or marriage.

The second call was from Headquarters Marine Corps. Earlier that year, I completed my master's degree in Human Resources Management and sent in the certification. I had not yet received transfer orders but was slated to go to Kansas City, Missouri, as the Recruiting Officer: my planned next assignment. Kansas City, Missouri was one of the most challenging areas of the country to recruit in, I had been told. There had been so many Marines from that State, a very patriotic state, killed during the Korean and Vietnam Wars. My monitor asked if I would like to go to the University of Washington for three years as the Marine Officer Instructor with the Naval R.O.T.C. program. That was where I attended university. I was delighted. Another miracle! These two wonderful calls verified God's favor and that what I had witnessed the previous night was real and genuine. I was not crazy! I had not imagined it. I was a devoted Roman Catholic at the time. I had read God sometimes communicates through visions but never expected one or heard from a friend about receiving one.

8

I began to pour through the Bible with a divine thirst. The first time I shared this life-changing vision was a year and a half after it happened. I was no longer brand new in this new brotherhood. I had developed trusted friends. One night I approached the invited Christian speaker at a Full Gospel Businessman's Fellowship International monthly banquet. It was in downtown Seattle. I told him what had happened to me and asked if he knew of anyone who had experienced something similar. He told me he knew of one person. Two months later, I approached another banquet speaker. He also said yes but said it was quite rare to have such a powerful visitation.

How did I come to join this worldwide organization of born-again believers I never knew existed until after my transformation? I would say it was a divine appointment with the Vice President of the Seattle Chapter of the FGBMFI. His name was John Andor. He became a great friend. This fellowship was well known outside traditional Catholic circles. John invited my family and me to the monthly banquet, where I heard a fantastic testimony of how God had transformed a successful businessman. I learned much about spiritual power. And what God was doing through men to spread the gospel. You might say I grew up spiritually with the help of this dynamic band of brothers. It was exciting looking forward weekly to a breakfast, luncheon, or dinner time with excited, motivated brothers in the LORD. Hearing life-changing testimonies of what God was doing in individuals and families fed my spirit and emboldened me in Christ. To be around, people genuinely excited about the gospel of Jesus Christ was new and refreshing. The men came from many different denominational backgrounds. It opened a whole new world I knew nothing about. The Bible became an exciting life changing book for me. It was no longer just a reference manual like a dictionary: to be used occasionally. It became a daily companion full of revelations!

the power of intercession

What in particular, did I learn from the vision? Certainly, it was a time of intimacy with Jesus Christ and that he loves me! I am still learning from it. I witnessed the Son of God in intercession for us on behalf of our Father in heaven. Was he responding to the prayers of faith from his saints around the world? Is he moving angels to counter what the devil is trying to accomplish? Is he speaking divine declarations into different situations in response to cries for help? All this and more!To be motivated to follow his example of intercession, one must have a different kind of faith than I had the first half of my life. Such a faith does not do well on an undernourished spiritual diet, so my understanding was anemic at best. My early faith was childlike, to be frank. Ignorance! Certainly not the God kind of faith that makes all the difference in life's varied and challenging situations. Up to the time of the vision, my faith was more faith in man using his natural talents wisely what he can do on his own. I had no idea of the benefits of true surrender to God! I had no real understanding of the power of the divine word or the authority of the Name of Jesus in prayer. I did not understand the clash behind the scenes between God's angels and Satan's fallen angels and how it affected my family and me. Or how it relates to human affairs! I had no practical understanding of how demons can and do influence men and women's actions or that troubling familiar spirits follow down through family bloodlines. I had grown up going to church on Sundays. So how could I have been so ignorant spiritually?

Jesus' warning of deception

I was in deception as a practicing believer in Jesus Christ. What a troubling thought. Scripture tells us, *"Jesus is the way, the truth, and the life..." (John 14:6)*. We see in scripture that when John, the Baptist, was in captivity and before his beheading, he sent a few of his disciples to Jesus to ask him if he was really the one, they were looking for. We see Jesus' response:

"Then Jesus answering said unto them, Go your way and tell John what things ye have seen and heard; how that the blind see, the lame walk, the lepers are cleansed, the deaf hear, the dead are raised, to the poor the gospel is preached. And blessed is he; whosoever shall not be offended in me."
~Luke 7: 22-23

In this passage, we see John the Baptist, examining himself in a challenging situation to see if he is in the faith. My scriptural challenge to those who believe! If we have grown up in a particular Christian religious experience, can we be sure we are walking in the complete faith that ensures the Lord's favor simply because of church doctrines and rituals we have attempted to practice faithfully? Shouldn't we set aside time occasionally to examine if we be in the faith? Personally, I believe because of the world situation and the length of time since the first coming of Jesus to the earth that we are at the door of his second coming. Because of his warning about the situation at that appointed time and about not being deceived, something more than our daily routines must be required of us. The word *"deception"* is used 74 times in scripture. No one, no matter how others esteem them, should take this warning lightly.

*"And Jesus answering them began to say, Take heed lest any man deceive you: For many shall come in my name, saying, I am Christ; and shall deceive many. ~" **Mark 13:5-7***

Just because a pastor acknowledges Jesus Christ as LORD does not mean he might not be off base, deceived and deceiving his congregation wrongly in some areas. An internet pastor said something interesting about the times we live in:

*"Much of what we are seeing around the world is a globalist show. ~" **Tim Henderson***

Jesus clearly warned us to trust no man. That certainly includes secular Mainstream Media and our other trusted institutions of learning in these increasingly evil times. He warned us about false prophets and teachers. Could some of what we have learned as Americans be distorted in different ways by evil people embedded inside our trusted institutions? Could some ideas we have learned be throwing us off course in life? How many of these leaders are walking in their own spiritual blindness? How can we be wary of others if we are not even examining ourselves?

And what kind of an examination is it if our standard isn't the written word of God? Concerning the final world leader: look what scripture says about him in **Daniel 11**. Though we cannot be certain who he is until after our departure (the rapture), can't you just feel he is somewhere alive on the earth?

"And the king shall do according to his will; and he shall exalt himself, and magnify himself above every god, and shall speak marvelous things against the God of gods and shall prosper till the indignation be accomplished: for that that is determined shall be done." ~**Daniel 11:36**

an authentic testimony

If one is truly born again, he will have a testimony of personal change worth listening to. I grew up going to church every Sunday. Over the years, I learned quite a few facts about how Christians should behave. I disciplined myself to follow accepted practices. I became comfortable with religious experiences and rituals. I thought I was a good person and on my way to heaven. Thank God all during that time, the Father was drawing me. Because of a certain emptiness that religion never filled, the familiar religious rituals and ceremonies never seemed quite enough. No matter what I learned, accomplished, or discovered I was never fully satisfied for long. I was in a spiritual search but didn't think of it that way. I was hesitant to share my faith. I did not have an exciting, transforming testimony that would convince others I was on the right religious path. I did not witness to others about my faith. Steve Quayle, a searcher, and researcher extraordinary said it this way:

"A witness has to really see something to have a valid testimony." ~**Steve Quayle**

Until the Lord turned my life upside down at the age of 39, I was mostly ignorant spiritually. Sure, I had some war stories from Vietnam, but no valid, meaningful testimony. Like most others, my identity was in my personal accomplishments, positions, titles, awards, and good works. No good deeds of our own can save us. Just the finished work of Jesus Christ at the Cross!

"For whosoever shall call upon the name of the Lord shall be saved." ~**Romans 10:13**

I am challenged to look at my heavenly communications from the standpoint *of real faith. Doing this means I need to examine myself in the light of* scripture to see if I be in the faith. What is the real state of my communion with God? The Bible says those who are his hear his voice.

"My sheep hear my voice and I know them, and they follow me: And I give unto them eternal life; and they shall never perish. ~" **John 10: 3-4, 27-28**

For the first half of my life, I was a religious person. I heard his written word proclaimed weekly. I can honestly tell you I never really heard his voice that I could be sure. I was comfortable in religion. I knew not to have fellowship with evil. But in my ignorance thought well of most people. I always gave others the benefit of the doubt. I really did not understand the hold evil can have on others and how they wear masks to deceive others. To a certain extent, I did keep separated from the world. I certainly was not attracted to obvious wrongdoing. I believed those who practiced Christianity were better off than those who were in spiritual darkness for sure. But I had little discernment of hidden evil.

the frightening rise of immorality

At this moment, we are not the great country we used to be. Morality has been turned on its head. If you are a thinking, discerning person, you will see the frightening rise of immorality. If you are an honest observer! I am shocked, however, at how undiscerning many nice people really are.

I appreciate what President Trump is trying to do to reverse the course of the deep state's death grip on America. It is shocking to hear seemingly decent people that don't respect his courageous efforts to reform this nation. Yes, he can be a bull in a China shop! But he needs the help of many to turn this nation around. Is it even possible now for any strong righteous man? Evil has penetrated deeply into our social fabric in my lifetime. I hope you find it as shocking as I do.

Civilizations and nations rise and fall as history demonstrates. In our generation, is something more going on here on earth than in prior ages? Are we that final generation? The one that will see the return of Jesus Christ to the earth? If that is the case, then a moral freefall worldwide is now happening that should alarm us. Is this what we are seeing? That it will happen at some point is biblical prophecy.

the restrainer

We know that the Restrainer spoken of in **II Thessalonians 2:7** is an actual person. He is still on the earth restraining the prophesized evil takeover of the antichrist. At some point, He (the Holy Spirit in born again believers) will be withdrawn (the Rapture). When that event happens, the United States for sure will be over as we know it.

Satan is a master of the takeover. We have seen great Christian institutions and great Christian hospitals, and great Christian movements started up and eventually became watered down spiritually. Why? Because of the corrupting power of evil! Most once righteous institutions become a secular shell of their former spiritual selves' overtime. A dynamic beginning certainly! But not now effecting the world for Christ as they first did. Think of how the Union Gospel Mission used to be in their heyday. Look what has happened to the Boy Scouts. Yes, there is a revival in parts of the world. We hear of one going on in China, Iran, and other persecuted nations. But much of what we hear of revival in the United States I have to wonder about. We have so perfected: glitz, lighting, hype, and musical performance. Is there genuine fear of the Lord, repentance, and humility underway, or have they just hyped-up events? If not, it is no real revival. If the Holy Ghost is not in charge, there can be no lasting fruit.

the truth about the present day

I do believe the time is running out to find out if we are in the faith. It has been about 2,000 years since the first coming of Jesus Christ. From Adam to Abraham was 2,000 years. From Abraham to Jesus, the same. On a seven-day layout of time, where a day is as a thousand years, we are near the beginning of the seventh day (the Millennial reign of Jesus Christ). I believe that the final Jubilee of the 120 years of Jubilees may have occurred in 2016. I think the time has about run out for us to make sure that we are in the faith.

Israel is our time clock to the prophetic countdown. Anyone who is situationally aware realizes that because Israel is back in the land as a nation (1948), the countdown clock is now ticking down. They recaptured Jerusalem. (1967) America moved our embassy to Jerusalem on May 14th, 2018. Russian, Iran, and Turkey, the main players in the coming Ezekiel 38-39 war, have moved into Syria on Israel's border. They have established their attack positions. It is prophesized Damascus (Isaiah 17:1) will soon become a ruinous heap! Israel is on high alert to do just that. Weapons of mass destruction are rumored to be stored under the city. The IDF could strike that city, the oldest on the earth, in a way that would ignite those stored weapons of mass destruction, ensuring they would never again become a city as prophesied in the Bible.

the time seems ripe

The time seems to be ripe for Father God to pull the trigger. What is the trigger? The soon coming rapture of the church! Researchers tell us that money in great amounts is being poured into developing the beast system that we see in the **Book of Revelation.** Every day somewhere in the news, we hear stories of gene splicing (Crisper technology), robotic developments, artificial intelligence, an evil use for the new 5G technology, space exploration, and so forth. **Daniel** tells us, such things will be true in the time of the end:

"But thou, O Daniel, shut up the words, and seal the book, even to the time of the end: many shall run to and fro, and knowledge shall be increased." ~Daniel 12:4

many are fast asleep

I understand the popularity of the argument of the liberals that we cannot sustain the population growth and must bring in a new world order to reduce the population. Thus, powerful nations like America need to subordinate themselves to this new order for the good of the world. But I disagree with this shortsighted globalist, antichrist position. They are ignorant that Bible prophecy predicts they will bring in their largely hidden agenda initiated by Rome's unelected Club founded in 1968 in Switzerland. I am on board with what President Trump is trying to accomplish to Make America Great Again. I support this effort. But the Bible does tell us the outcome of the President's efforts retraining can at best only postpone the Deep State's plan temporarily.

"And it was given unto him to make war with the saints and to overcome them: and power was given him over all kindreds, and tongues, and nations. And all that dwell upon the earth shall worship him, whose names are not

written in the book of life of the Lamb slain from the foundation of the world."
~Revelation 13:7-8

So, I ask you: Are your communications with God completely frank and honest? Are you sure you are secure in the faith? Are you really awake to what is coming on the earth? Are you rapture ready? In such a time as I am indicating we are in, godly communications is being fiercely resisted by the enemy of our souls. The spiritual warfare is increasingly vigorous! Satan's time is short, but he will get his day. If you are saying amen to this chapter and want more protection and fight to do what God intends for us to do in these final moments, then read on to get better equipped for the battle at hand.

"Behold, I stand at the door and knock. If any man hears my voice and opens the door, I will come into him, and will sup with him, and he with me. To him that overcometh will I grant to sit with me in my throne, even as I also overcame, and am set down with my Father in his throne." *~Revelation 3: 20-21*

And when he comes in its a shout aloud once in a lifetime kind of experience. At least it was for me. And there is something vitally important about reading scripture aloud. Your heart hears your mouth confessing it through your ears. It does something to one's being that doesn't happen to me when I read silently to myself. And the demons and God's angels who are watching are put on notice.

2

RATS IN THE CAMP

Some memories are genuine and lasting. This title
phrase instantly takes me back to 1969. The Army's 101st
Airborne Division was conducting an operation against the
enemy. They were the fighting division next to and south of
our division. General Richard Stillwell, USA, the Corps
Commander in northern South Vietnam, ordered a few Marine
units from the 3d Marine Division to occupy 101st Airborne
defensive positions vacated while they were out on their large-
scale offensive operation against the North Vietnamese army.
My rifle company was trucked down to an army fire support
base near their division base camp. I cannot remember its name
now. Too long ago! We trucked from near Dong Ha down to
the outskirts of Quang Tri, as I recall.

a story
After debarking my truck, the first thing I noticed
was two rats scampering around this hastily evacuated

defensive perimeter. At first glance, it seemed unkempt. It had an unsanitary overall look to it. Our mission was to occupy and provide security for this artillery fire support base for the next ten days. Trenches, bunkers, barbed wire would be our companions. Trash had been thrown out into the barbed wire beyond the perimeter! Either the last unit did not have good sanitary standards, or leadership was in a real hurry to move them out. This left us to do the cleanup. The trash barrels were packed to overflowing. Some of the men obviously had had dysentery problems. When the urge hit them, they could not get to the four holers on time to relieve themselves properly. The four holers hadn't been burned out before leaving, accounting for the unhealthy smell in the air. Lots of flies, mosquitos, and varmints were congregating. A lot like in certain areas of many of our liberal-controlled cities across America. A problem that is growing into a national scandal. (sanctuaries for who knows what kinds of rodents.) Humans taking a few steps out beyond their tents and relieving themselves wherever they please with no consequences for them. It is so sad to drive into downtown Seattle and by those streets that have been abandoned to such a spectacle.

I ordered our company Gunnery Sergeant to have the men do a sweep to clean up the place. We were not in the habit of leaving our living spaces in Vietnam in such poor shape. Though not ordered to do so, we had the time and means to clean up the mess and did so. Adequate sanitation is so critical to long term health. I can tell you it did not endear us to this particular army unit. I have no respect for the leadership of many of our mayors and city councils across America who are allowing such a state to grow and exist. Certainly not the wish of their hardworking, law-abiding citizens. My order to clean up the mess of others was not a popular order, so I personally joined in doing my share of the disgusting cleanup work— nothing worse than having to clean up someone else's crap. I remember as a non-smoker hating being ordered to clean up the butts of the smokers dropped on the ground during my boot camp days as a lowly recruit. I was then and still am today a non-smoker. Ugh! But it has to be done. Ours was a quiet time there and pleasant except for that awful first day.

reminds me of today

Why this story? It reminds me of a lot of situations increasing numbers of law-abiding citizens are now facing across America because of irresponsible political leadership. In America, we have an ever-growing number of communities opening their arms to undisciplined druggies because of poor leadership decisions. Treating them like functional citizens is no way to handle things. The great population centers with far greater resources at their disposal are now adversely affecting the smaller towns surrounding them as the down and outers they are hosting venture out into the surrounding territories. My town is just two hours from Seattle. The growing lawlessness in Seattle is now affecting our nice little town adversely because of their poor decision-making. Spreading messes, too long tolerated, such as Seattle's homeless camps, must be addressed nationally I believe. The problem is out of control for many smaller towns. Washington D. C. and our state capitols must step in where cities and towns have lost control. The lack of responsibility and accountability at senior levels in past administrations is now quite visible. It is time to institute some kind of national boot camp program to put vagrants living on our streets, in alleys, and city parks. They are vagrants and breaking so many laws and creating a growing slum.

I frankly wonder if this nation has the resolve to face the truth and tackle problems that can no longer be hidden. We all are witnessing it. An all-hands effort is needed to correct this problem. It's no longer someone else's problem but ours too. Is our cup of iniquity (**Jeremiah 16:18**) as a nation about full? Is Judgment at the door? Only the fear of God, as occurred in the ancient city of Ninevah when Jonah was sent by God to preach 40 days, then destruction will stay God's growing anger. I expect things can be turned around. But frankly, I do not see the fear of God across our land that is necessary to do so. The greater part of the church is still fast

21

asleep. Only such a fear would stay the hand of God's judgment if we are to believe scripture. He did it once before, so he would do it again.

"And the word of the LORD came unto Jonah the second time, saying, Arise, go unto Nineveh, that great city, and preach unto it the preaching that I bid thee. So, Jonah arose, and went unto Nineveh, according to the word of the LORD. Now Nineveh was an exceeding great city of three days' journey. And Jonah began to enter into the city a day's journey, and he cried and said Yet forty days, and Nineveh shall be overthrown. So, the people of Nineveh believed God, and proclaimed a fast, and put on sackcloth, from the greatest of them even to the least of them. For word came unto the king of Nineveh, and he arose from his throne, and he laid his robe from him, and covered him with sackcloth, and sat in ashes. And he caused it to be proclaimed and published through Nineveh by the decree of the king and his nobles, saying, let neither man nor beast, herd nor flock, taste anything: let them not feed, nor drink water: But let man and beast be covered with sackcloth, and cry mightily unto God: yea, let them turn every one from his evil way, and from the violence that is in their hands. Who can tell if God will turn and repent, and turn away from his fierce anger, that we perish not? And God saw their works, that they turned from their evil way; and God repented of the evil, that he had said that he would do unto them; and he did it not."

Jonah 3:1-10

Ignoring poor sanitation and not following standards on how to keep oneself healthy invites sickness and disease, resulting in future loss of manpower. It is a fight to stay healthy in any situation: especially where fighting and riots are going on. Losing people to disease can be just as grave a loss to an organization as members being wounded or killed. Crime should not be allowed to grow in urban areas because we feel bad for those who have less than us. Laws must be enforced while being compassionate to those who really deserve our help. Turning this nation around from its downward plunge toward the abys is a monumental task. I don't see right now that a significant number of millennials are up to it. It seems America has been infested with rats of the humankind. Cities have a bigger policing problem because they attract strangers, many with unrighteous spirits and unholy opinions and attitudes. We see real rebellion and stubbornness on display nightly in many of our urban communities bringing back the anti-war rioting during the 1960s.

This is a critical moment in history. We are at the brink, and too many ignorant do-nothings are in positions of power and authority and are not addressing the right issues, now reversing everything President Trump tried to do to make America great again. Thank God for a short time we did have a president who was opposing and attempting to weed out these destructive behaviors. But will enough of us wake up and support him in the short time we have left, or is it too late? So, what can the average person who cares do? Certainly, pray and begin attacking near at hand problems he or she sees that are doable.

illegal immigrants

Most of us can't help tackling the national problems we see in any direct way. Yes, there are some terrible hombres among those coming north across our southern border. Think MS-13 gang members and sleeper cells from terrorist nations. The news today as I write (November 5, 2019) is about a Mormon family ambushed and butchered in Mexico. Trump's reported reaction? *"It's time to take on the cartels."* This reminds me of the third peril in the Prophecy of George Washington to come upon America. (see the last chapter of this book.) A vision of our national future? The third peril of that vision is a physical attack against America that almost overcomes us. What is happening to us now seems to me to describe such perilous times.

The latest news article estimated the number of illegal immigrants crossing our southern border count at 22 million. But there is a positive side to this. Think of the many babies aborted over the last 40 plus years since the terrible Roe vs. Wade Supreme Court decision (50 million?) by our citizens. I wonder if God in his mercy has sent north a lot of good people in desperate circumstances to replace those who were aborted in violation of God's ordinances to give us a chance to redeem ourselves as a nation. Most Hispanics are decent, hard-working people and a credit to our nation. Illegal immigration can be seen as a potential blessing if handled in a godly manner. The Bible tells us to treat the strangers in our midst in a decent fashion. This is God's desire. So far, the results of our national behavior toward them is mixed. It is a shame we have to spend money out of our own pockets on their schooling and medical expenses and such. But if our own aborted babies had all lived, we would have spent a similar amount to support and raise them. Yes, too many who come north are not nice people making the lives of their neighbors difficult. Our border security must be tightened, and President Trump was doing that as fast as he could in difficult times. My wife found that out when she served for eighteen months on the Yakima Grand Jury.

Why do so many illegals come north? Of course, for a better life for them and their families! Parts of their own nations they flee from are filled with corruption and violence. They are being let down by many of their national leaders. It is happening to us now, here in sanctuary cities across America, in violation of existing laws and expectations. The deep state plans to reduce us through illegal immigration and other illicit means to force us into their New World Order. Why does this situation exist? Why haven't prior administrations and Congresses done something to take control before Trump? I smell a rat! Is God giving us one last chance with President Trump? Or is he sounding the Trumpet of God using Trump as a final warning to wake us up to the nearness of the biblically prophesized coming Great Tribulation? Yes! And yes! Why humans who act like rats end up in control in government is not a mystery. They do it by lying, cheating, and stealing from gullible people. It's the nature of rats! Too many of us are way too naive. We are letting them overrun our communities in the name of kindness, tolerance, and political correctness.

*"This known also, that in the last days perilous times shall come. For men shall be lovers of their own selves, covetous, boasters, proud, blasphemers, disobedient to parents, unthankful, unholy, Without natural affection, trucebreakers, false accusers, incontinent, fierce, despisers of those that are good, Traitors, heady, high-minded, lovers of pleasures more than lovers of God; Having a form of godliness, but denying the power thereof: from such turn away. For of this sort are they which creep into houses, and lead captive silly women laden with sins, led away with divers' lusts, Ever learning, and never able to come to the knowledge of the truth." ~2 **Timothy 3:1-7**

This passage speaks to the character of many in leadership today. More Americans need to wake up and fight spiritually and physically to help control our society. The God-given ability to fight on all fronts allowed us in three and a half years to overcome both Japan and Germany during the Second World War. Many more of us used to have that kind of fight than today. Why is this? The millennials need to find the real answer to that question because God's prophetic clock is winding down, and they have the most to lose.

*"For he bringeth down them that dwell on high; the lofty city, he layeth it low; he layeth it low, even to the ground; he bringeth it even to the dust. The foot shall tread it down, even the feet of the poor, and the steps of the needy."~ **Isaiah 26:5**

society grows corruption

Many still question whether there is a deep state running our nation behind closed doors while many in Congress play-act at leading. It is hard to believe this could really be so. But seriously, analyze what has happened to us in the past 40 years! The decline I have witnessed in my adult lifetime shows me much of what goes on in our state capitols and Washington D.C. are staged.

A takeover and takedown are in progress! The above scriptural passage confirms this. And God is letting it happen! The passage is so descriptive it bears repeating:

"This also know that in the last days, perilous times shall come. For men shall be lovers of their own selves, covetous, boasters, proud, blasphemers, disobedient to parents, unthankful, unholy, Without natural affection, trucebreakers, false accusers, incontinent, fierce, despisers of those that are good, Traitors, heady, high-minded, lovers of pleasures more than lovers of God; Having a form of godliness, but denying the power thereof: from such turn away. For of this sort are they which creep into houses, and lead captive silly women laden with sins, led away with divers lusts, Ever learning, and never able to come to the knowledge of the truth." ***2 Timothy 3: 1-7***

Who is too slow-witted to see that our Mainstream Media pundits are daily reading off of identical, prepared scripts? Told what to report and what not to report! Some clever observer recently said, *"MSM is all about under-reporting, misreporting and not reporting."* For things to be as messed up as they are in many parts of America, certainly some of the people we elect and send to our nation's capital must not be doing their jobs honestly based on the oath they took to represent us. They must be being bribed or blackmailed. We are being overcome by the evil within. Not enough of our elected leaders are really making a difference. Corruption is widespread and eating away the fabric of our institutions. I would ask: Have you heard from your pastor any end time scriptures? Are we that terminal generation spoken of in Scripture? If he never preaches from the prophetic passages, he is part of the problem, not the solution. If the situation is as grave as I think it is, why have we as a nation not yet been judged by God? I believe for one big reason. Our support of Israel!

"And I will bless them that bless thee, and curse him that curseth thee: and in thee shall all families of the earth be blessed;" ~Genesis 12:3

the D.C. swamp

President Trump was the most pro-Israel president ever elected. Look at the evil going on right under our noses: abortions, child trafficking, pornography, greed, murder, treason, corrupt judges, bribery, political blackmail, removal of prayer from the public square, public lying, etc. President Trump accused Obama of treason, and there is growing evidence this is so. Yet half our nation is represented as adoring Obama. How can this be? Judicial Watch has made a strong case he is guilty of treason. Is he waiting in the wings to step back in power through a coup? Could he be the coming antichrist? If you think this is farfetched, review all the dreams, visions, teachings, and hard evidence posted on the internet.

History shows Spain turned their back on Israel. That betrayal put their nation, a world power at the time, into a serious decline. England turned their back on Israel. It then lost most of its overseas empire, and was no longer the world power. Germany turned its back on Israel. Hitler was the result. They are now being overrun by Islam. America has not officially turned its back yet. But many of our citizens are showing a disposition to support a leader who would do just that. President Trump is at present acting as a modern-day Cyrus in his help toward Israel. We are blessed as a result, in spite of all the evil in our midst. Read the book, The Oracle. It discusses this blessing-cursing relationship with Israel. I read where President Trump ordered (Oct 2019) the federal agencies to stop subscribing to the New York Times and the Washington Post because of their vary biased reporting. Their lies have gotten worse over time—what a shame. Our president was trying to drain the swamp in Washington D. C. as he promised to do if elected. Look at the constant resistance he experienced within his own administration at the career bureaucrat level. Is it possible for him, even with four more years, to turn things around so we will return to simpler times? Because of the heavy educational and media brainwashing of the younger generations against our traditional values, I seriously doubt it!

The outcome of the 2020 elections is disputed. Will America go the way of all other once-great nations? Americans who leaned toward the conservative point of view are now seeing a new administration scrap everything he has attempted to do. They will then attempt to do to us what they have attempted to do to President Trump since 2016! The Jews and the nation of Israel will certainly need to brace themselves. I know there are some very evil Jews. Most Jews are still blinded spiritually concerning their true Messiah. Many still reject Jesus Christ. Many secretly despise Christians. I know this. Even so, we are to pray for the peace of Jerusalem (**Psalms 122:6**) and bless those who hate us.

Leviticus

During ancient times and into the middle ages, people knew very little about disease. Except for Israel! God gave them strict sanitary and hygiene rules in the Bible. That is a major reason they could overcome the giants. Better nutrition! The lack of knowledge of what to eat and not to eat weakened their enemies. Why did God choose Israel to bless? The Bible tells us why. Because they were the smallest and the least of the peoples of the world, he did not choose them because they were any better than the people around them. We see many of these dietary practices in the book of Leviticus. The word rat is not found in the King James Bible. But *Leviticus 11:29* certainly mentions the class of things that crawl on the ground that are their cousins.

"These also shall be unclean unto you among the creeping things that creep upon the earth, the weasel, and the mouse, and the tortoise after his kind, And the ferret, and the chameleon, and the lizard, and the snail, and the mole. These are unclean to you among all that creep: whosoever doth touch them, when they be dead, shall be unclean until the even."

Such creatures were invisible disease carriers. The Jews had God's word, which steeled those who followed God's dictates. The surrounding nations, enemies of Israel, had no such protection. This is still true today for those who don't study the Bible and heed its instructions. Most nations have Jews in their midst who have not returned to the promised land. In the surrounding nations encompassing Jerusalem, Jews who are conspicuous are killed. Islam does its best to keep such hatred alive. Now they are infiltrating and corrupting many of our institutions across America and western civilization. Why the Muslim Brotherhood has not been declared a terrorist organization is anyone's guess. But presently, we are still like a big brother to Israel.

curses

Most of us are concerned about our personal health, some more than others. A symptom develops! We wonder what is causing it. When I was younger, I just assumed it would go away. Most of the time, it did. A headache, a chest pain, a spasm in my leg! We who look to God pray and believe, and the healing begins. In the last few years, doctors have begun to advertise their clinics, medical associations, and pharmaceutical corporations. These ads, in my view, are a form of brainwashing. I hate the effect it has had on all age groups. Many who once looked to God now rush to their doctor for any little thing. Medical ads plant the question: *"if you have this or that symptom, you might have this. Consult your doctor."* This was not true for much of my life.

The most godless secular systems have trained up a generation of younger people who are conditioned to show no patience or endurance and believe whatever the so-called experts tell them. Many run to the doctor with every little ache and pain. They have no understanding of the fact that our immune system is a self-healing work of God. Or that God does answer healing prayers! Even if some do believe this, they have little or no patience to give God time. They pray for God to answer their prayer and immediately schedule an appointment showing their lack of faith in their prayer. On top of this, the economic system we live in pushes on us genetically modified foods that even rats refuse to eat. And the public water systems: who knows what is in the water these days? Probably not good either! Can we trust all bottled water companies? And the air: can the chemicals they are spraying in the sky (Chem-trails) be good for our lungs or crops or animals in the fields? Who do you trust more: God or man?

We find the word curse 187 times in the Bible. Curses are real. They enable evil people to hurt others, but we must give them power through agreement. How do we do this? Sin, fear, and unbelief open the doors for these curses to come in! We know our God is a God of blessing. (**Genesis 49:25**) Our God is a protector. But curses are like fiery darts.

"Above all, taking the shield of faith, wherewith ye shall be able to quench all the <u>fiery darts</u> *of the wicked."*
~Ephesians 6:16

So, what is the result? Most Christians can't get a hold of divine promises like those found in **Psalm 91**. Very sad! Early in 2020, we saw the coronavirus come out of China. Most likely a deep state effort. Americans should not be living in fear but declaring wonderful promises of God over their lives, such as in **Psalm 91: 5-7**

"Thou shalt not be afraid for the terror by night; nor for the arrow that flieth by day; Nor for <u>the pestilence</u> *that walketh in darkness; nor for the destruction that wasteth at noonday. A thousand shall fall at thy side, and ten thousand at thy right hand; but* <u>it shall not come nigh thee."</u>

a supernatural principle
The word of God tells us:

*"Death and life are in the power of the tongue, and they that love it shall eat the fruit thereof." ~**Proverbs 18:21***

Are you choosing life or death in your everyday decisions and communications? As I write this sentence, we are close to Halloween night! Those who celebrate this particular day are, for the most part, fun-loving. But anyone who thinks about what is behind this occasion will realize it promotes a culture of death and horror. The innocent need to be very wary on such a night. Those without a habit of prayer should be cautious. Jesus Christ talking with the Roman centurion in **Matthew 8:13,** knew the power of words of faith:

" For if ye live after the flesh, ye shall die: but if ye through the Spirit do mortify the deeds of the body, ye shall live. "

He said we need to bring our bodies into subjection for the fruits of living faith to become evident. Jesus taught much about the power of the tongue. On the importance of our confession! On matters of faith, his words need to be memorized. There is real power in a living faith. Most of us grownups are still babies when it comes to appropriating help from the supernatural realm where our Father lives. Why? Because we were raised to be self-reliant and independent. And stubborn too!

"And Peter calling to remembrance saith unto him, Master, behold, the fig tree which thou <u>cursed</u> is withered away. And Jesus answering saith unto them, Have faith in God. For verily I say unto you, That whosoever shall say unto this mountain, Be thou removed, and be thou cast into the sea; and shall not doubt in his heart, but shall believe that those things which he saith shall come to pass; <u>he shall have whatsoever he saith</u>. " ~Mark 11:21-23

We know because the Bible says it that every word of scripture is God-breathed. In this world, we are told that there will be tribulation. We all need supernatural help more than we realize. It is promised by God to those who believe. When we are attacked, no matter how, we can call for our heavenly

Father's help and expect Him to respond. I love the Word of God. Since I have discovered how wicked the world really is; and how many human rats are walking among us even in the daylight, not counting after darkness falls, it has caused me to be much more alert and prayerful. I am not trusting of man the way I once was. Especially the ones who call themselves professionals!

God gives us availability to his power in heaven and on earth. How many believers have read the **Book of Job**, or even heard it preached from the pulpit? Scholars tell us it may be the oldest book in the Bible. It was written long before the first coming of Christ. Certainly, before the promise of the Father (the Holy Spirit) was sent to the earth to indwell his believers! Look at the below promise. I have personally never heard it mentioned from the pulpit on a Sunday morning.

*"Thou shall also decree a thing, and it shall be established unto thee, and the light shall shine upon thy ways." ~ **Job 22:28***

What a promise! When you need to call on God for help, this implies real authority to do so. Where does the power to decree come from? God tells us. We, who are the Father's children, are told to pray to Him in the Name of Jesus Christ. We have been given the authority to use that wonderful name.

*"That at the name of Jesus every knee should bow, of things in heaven, and things in earth, and things under the earth; And that every tongue should confess that Jesus Christ is Lord, to the glory of God the Father." ~**Philippians 2:10-11***

Halloween night

My wife and I like to go for drives. We drove through a neighborhood in our small town and saw that one house had been decorated for the upcoming Halloween night. I am not exaggerating! They had spent thousands of dollars on items that were spread all over their yard and porch. I have never seen anything like it in a neighborhood. Maybe Disneyland might have such a display. But in the small town of Ellensburg? Who does that? And for the scariest night of the year? Someone very naive or very dark. Certainly, with a very different world view than I have!

One of our favorite places to visit is the town of Leavenworth, Washington: a mountain town. Seven million tourists a year visit this small mountain town an hour away. They have a Christmas shop that is open year-round. Maybe 20 years ago, it opened up a Halloween section. It is not yet as big as what they sell for Christmas displays. But I expect it will at some point become larger. There is a real move toward the dark side throughout the world. This enterprise is in a Christian run town. So many are turning back to the paganism that existed before the first visit of Jesus Christ to the earth. The owners have been forced to cater to those who love Halloween to stay in business! A sad commentary! A definite sign we are in the last days. Jonathan Kahn, in his latest best-seller: The Oracle, which is about the biblical Jubilee cycle, explains this trend away from goodness back to unrightiousness; and why this is a real happening right now. An excellent read!

I am shocked at the general public's interest in the culture of death across America. The Bible prophesies this will happen. Those who are aware see it coming to pass at lightning speed. At the same time, we see a trend in the church away from teaching any prophecy at all—no warning to their flock about the things to come. Many pastors teach only what is popular. What helps their church to grow! Tickling ears is the trend in much of the church these days. Too many don't want to hear scriptural truth. What happened to preaching to change hearts with the gospel? Discussing biblical prophecy is apparently too challenging for many pastors in this age of political correctness. Are there rats in the church too? I think so. But there are many decent people in the institutional church. They just need to start speaking out.

age of the super-soldier

The Epstein story of corruption in high places has broken wide open. Americans who want the truth have learned of the blackmail of key leaders going on. The vehicle is child trafficking; Hollywood is deeply connected, and so too are many of the elites in every strata of society. The infestation of human rats has become more and more obvious to those of us who are not hardened against believing such evil exists. It has corrupted people in many of the various civilian chains of command across America. The sealed indictments compiled during the Trump Administration have, thankfully, grown. Over 222,000 at the start of 2021. They can be released at the most strategic time, which must be soon if this effort isn't somehow stopped by the Deep State. President Trump, I think, invoked the Insurrection Act before leaving DC and turned power over to the military due to the fraudulent election. The declass will come if he gets another four-year term in office. Could the rapture happen first? The Jason Bourne series hints at the level of technology available to those in control. It is becoming unreal, but it is real. A growing number of citizens are ready to believe almost any story except God's story in the Bible.

How is it even possible for the average person to stand against such high tech evil when turned against an identified enemy? It brought a connected and righteous man, Roger Stone, to his knees. With his pardon, he is now openly thanking God. He was for certain on his way to prison, a death sentence if President Trump had not intervened. It isn't possible in the natural to overcome such evil. No matter how sharp, talented, and good one is, such a person will be overcome without God's divine help. Most of us are born with far less capability than those who were straight A+ students from K through 12 and university. I know a few that never cracked a textbook. Is there help from God for those of us who are just average?

The good news is yes! Divine help is available and can even the odds or beat the odds. I am living proof of that.

"I returned, and saw under the sun, that the race is not to the swift, nor the battle to the strong, neither yet bread to the wise, nor yet riches to men of understanding, nor yet favour to men of skill; but time and chance happeneth to them all." ~*Ecclessiastes 9:11*

"Because the foolishness of God is wiser than men; and the weakness of God is stronger than men." ~*I Corinthians 1:25*

The Bible tells those who read it: *"When we cast our cares on him, he will care for us."* The important question is: Will we cast our cares on Him? I have, and this book is my testimony that God is an ever-present help to such as really surrender their lives to him.

My wife and I met with a male friend for breakfast recently. His parents are dead. He is like a son. We have known him for about a decade. He has a wife and two small children. He married later in life. We met him when he was single. It is the first marriage for both he and his wife. He is about ten years older than his wife, who is 40. It is not easy to be married and raise small children with all the challenges faced without supporting parents and grandparents. We have many lonely people who could disciple those who are amongst us, struggling alone. We all come into this world hard-wired to be who we are. We all come into a marriage with expectations that can smack our spouse in the face. We listen, give advice, and encourage him in his walk and his wife, too. And we are finding we are more blessed than they by the relationship.

My wife has an interesting perspective on the human struggle. She was given up for adoption as a baby. She had an amazing relationship with her dad growing up. She said to our friend at breakfast that she never fit into the family she was placed with, given her different DMA structure. At the age of 41, she met her biological mother. For the first time, everything made sense. She saw why she had to fight off certain tendencies to act in certain ways. Why she felt mostly alone in the extended family she was placed in. Why she never really fit in. Until she surrendered her life to Christ in her 30s and started getting supernatural support from above, she was just the way she was.

closing thoughts

Do you see how hard-wired each of us is! We seem driven to go down certain paths! It is hard, if not impossible, to change ourselves. Certainly, even harder to change others! We will not ever change unless we surrender and let God, who wants and can help, into our lives to help us change! It is He who gives us the life-changing power we all desperately need.

"There is a way that seemeth right to a man, but the ends there of are the ways of death."
~**Proverbs 14:12**

How do we survive at all in this world that is heading in the wrong direction with increasing speed? We cannot turn the world around according to the Bible. Without divine help we too are lost. But divine power is available to all who surrender to the One who controls it all. We have varying degrees of spiritual influence in the lives of others through effective prayer. Only a person can change themselves. We all need outside help to do this. Our most significant power over others is through effective prayer and example.

Are there one or more rats in your camp? Be it home, job, or community? Is there someone standing in the way of your success and happiness? Are you at odds with people who should love and appreciate you? Is it time to cry out to the only one who can help in this fallen world? His name? Jesus Christ of Nazareth. He is the Breaker. (**Micah 2:13**) And some of those who mistreat us need to be broken.

The Bible clearly shows when sin enters the camp, the whole army is weakened. (**Joshua 7**) It is a passage worth reading: it tells how one man named Achan weakened the whole army of Israel, how Joshua had to deal with this problem. Or it would be the downfall of all Israel, the nation. Read about Achan's trespass in the Book of Joshua. Its effect on Israel! Not dealing with our rats at every level <u>will</u> take down this nation. Don't let it take down you, too.

3

AUTHORITY AND POWER

We all appeal to some power or authority greater than us. There are significant life challenges where we cannot make it without the help of others. Babies appeal to parents. They need to be fed, bathed, changed, burped, and loved on, for starters. Have you heard the scripture verse:

"He that spareth his rod hateth his son: but he that loveth him chasteneth him betimes."
~**Proverbs 13:24**

Where does our focus need to be while raising children? What is the common denominator between your baby image and the uncivil rioters we see raging on many of our streets across the nation in the evening news? There are many out of control adults who have never experienced the love of correction from a parent at home during their growing years and now are now having temper tantrums as young adults. The battle for control starts almost right away at birth. If this need for control is not channeled in a good direction early, it will not be good for society. This need is inherent in our human nature.

Many households have lost this battle with their baby before the age of five. What is now happening on our streets is one of the results.

All "power" and "authority" flow from God. Power to overcome obstacles is available from those in authority over us. Everyone in the various chains of command that believers deal with has a certain degree of power at various levels of authority to address particular challenges citizens face. Looking back over my life, I now see that before my eyes were opened, I sometimes was overcome where help was available because I was too independent to ask for help. I just had to find the right source to request help. But I sometimes didn't—a*ll* **"power"** and *"authority" flow from God.* Power to overcome obstacles is a challenge we all face. In some situations, we do not have the personal strength or intellect to overcome the obstacles facing us. Not having enough personal power or influence in a situation where we are responsible and not asking a senior for available help is not wise. God wants his children to live a victorious, abundant life. He is adept at helping us, his family, work through setbacks and missteps. Many who confess Christ never walk in the power and authority that God desires for them. This is really sad. I wish I could say I have never fallen short, but I can't. I can say that God was always there when I fell to help me to get back on my feet. He has been good to me all the time. But too often, I did not realize it at the time. We all have also experienced roadblocks in the chains of command.

The word power is used 281 times in God's written word. We find the word authority used 46 times. Let us look at authority first. For the sake of time, I will skip past some of these Bible verses.

Esther 9:29 *"Then Esther the queen, the daughter of Abihail, and Mordecai the Jew, wrote with all* authority *to confirm this second letter of Purim."*

The first thing I see about the word "authority" here is the word author inside the word. What does an author do but write? Who will read his or her writings

if they do not convey a sense of authority and power? This is why sacred literature has more impact than secular writings when one's spiritual eyes are opened. Therefore, Satan does his best to keep us from what we need to see and hear. He tries to deny us the understanding we need to overcome.

Who and what gives authors the power to write successful works? Certainly, the experience is part of it. With experience should come credibility. But most importantly, if one is to write with power, there must be wisdom and revelation from on high. This can only come from one greater than us. What we write must be bathed in prayer, or there will be no real anointing (or help from God) concerning what we write. Just another clever or not so clever book, article, or column! It's the anointing (or favor of God) that makes all the difference in life.

Why is the first use of this word found in the Book of Esther? Read the whole chapter and see. Esther is placed in a position of influence to save God's people. Observe what God put Esther through before giving her position and authority. Look at what happened to the prior queen. She lacked wisdom from above and was removed from being queen. This change had critical ramifications. Not just for Esther, but also for all her people.

"When the righteous are in authority *the people rejoice: but when the wicked beareth rule, the people mourn."~ Proverbs 29:2*

The above two verses are the only verses in the Old Testament using this important word. I asked myself why? When you go to the New Testament, you see why. Throughout the Old Testament, we see kings and generals who craved and wielded massive authority and power. Men with life and death rule over others! It is a wonder this word was only used twice. Until you see who comes on to the scene in a visible way in the New Testament; the one who has all authority. God himself in the human form of Jesus Christ! There is power in his Name. But few believers use it effectively because of ignorance.

> *"For he taught them as one having <u>authority</u> and not as the scribes."* ~ **Matthew 7:29**

All authority points to God either directly or indirectly. If you want authority, the only real way is through surrender to one who is above you who can delegate such authority. I confess to you as one human being to another that surrender is the last thing I wanted to do. It isn't just truly deceived people, witches and warlocks and the like, who look to themselves. It seems to be in the D.N.A. of all of us. We do not want to surrender. So, surrendering is required all throughout the various chains of command to the authorities above, and this is not an easy thing for us to do. We are all blind as bats in a spiritual sense in the daytime though we think we can see. Really evil people work their evil deeds even in daylight. And yes, they are under Satan's authority! Often the anointing you feel is a satanic one. Beware! Most do not know this, but Satan grants power you don't want to gain because of the price that comes with it: eternal damnation!

spiritual authority

What do natural authority and the chain of command have to do with spiritual authority? Everything! We all have our own unique experiences that produce a definite focus in our lives over time. Or, in some cases, a lack of focus! My experiences are somewhat unique only because, so few children are born into a military family and then go on to join the military and make it their profession too. I had a very different early life and young adult experience compared with that of most. My habits and expectations were developed or influenced because of this rather uncommon upbringing. Of course, we are all the same in many ways having the same human nature.

Can my perspective help you? A good question. Sometimes a different set of eyes can help open things up for someone in a rut or pit if they will truly listen with their heart. The need to understand spiritual warfare and become adept at fighting in the spirit realm is not unique to my life. Satan, his fallen angels, and demons hate you just as much as they hate me. Therefore, we all need supernatural help. But civilians rarely think about daily life from a warfare perspective, especially in a blessed nation like America. We all must learn how to fight in the invisible realm, or we, too, will perish. It helped me tremendously when I finally realized the similarities between natural and spiritual warfare. That understanding can help you also.

Civilian public schools do not teach students how to fight. They try to teach something quite different from military training. Mostly how to out nice those who do not treat others in a civil manner, and if that doesn't work, call 911! Your first response when someone takes unfair advantage of you may be to summon someone in natural authority to help you. You have been warned not to defend yourself. That is discouraged because it can lead to legal difficulties.

All of us have supernatural enemies. Most, while aware of humans who do not like them, are unaware of what is going on in the supernatural realm. The side you are on ultimately determines whether you win or lose. The Bible challenges believers to have *"ears to hear and eyes to see,"* meaning we need to take our blinders off to gain a godly perspective. Our perspective should be different from the worlds! Thinking of men in authority, I think of the many great men, some very terrible, who impacted history. Some alive, many passed on. I like history. Take Joshua, a great Old Testament figure, for instance. I have tried to memorize some of his holy declarations.

the mantle passes to Joshua

"Now after the death of Moses, the servant of the LORD, it came to pass that the LORD spake unto Joshua the son of Nun, Moses' minister, saying, Moses, my servant is dead; now, therefore, go over this Jordan, thou, and all this people unto the land which I do give to them, even to the children of Israel. Every place that the soul of your foot shall tread upon that have I given unto you, as I said unto Moses. From the wilderness and this Lebanon even unto the great river, the river Euphrates, all the land of the Hittites, and unto the great sea toward the going down of the sun, shall be your coast. There shall not any man be able to stand before thee all the days of your life: as I was with Moses, so I will be with thee: I will not fail thee, nor forsake thee. Be strong and of a good courage: for unto this people shall thou divide for an inheritance the land which I swore unto their fathers to give them. Only be thou strong and very courageous, that thou mayest observe to do according to all the law, which Moses my servant commanded thee: turn not from it to the right hand or to the left, that thou mayest prosper whithersoever thou goest. This book of the law shall not depart out of thy mouth; but thou shalt meditate therein day and night, that thou mayest observe to do according to all that is written therein: for then thou shall make thy way prosperous, and then thou shalt have good success. Have not I commanded thee? Be strong and of a good courage; be not afraid, neither be thou dismayed: for the LORD thy God is with thee whithersoever thou goest. Then Joshua commanded the officers of the people, saying, Pass through the host, and command the people, saying, Prepare you victuals; for within three days you shall pass over this Jordan, to go in to possess the land which the LORD your God giveth you to possess it. And to the Reubenites, and to the Gadites, and to half the

*tribe of Manasseh, spake Joshua, saying, Remember the word which Moses the servant of the LORD commanded you, saying, The LORD your God hath given you rest and hath given you this land. Your wives, your little ones, and your cattle shall remain in the land which Moses gave you on this side Jordan; but ye shall pass before your brethren armed, all the mighty men of valor, and help them; Until the LORD have given your brethren rest, as he hath given you, and they also have possessed the land which the LORD your God giveth them: then ye shall return unto the land of your possession, and enjoy it, which Moses the LORD'S servant gave you on this side Jordan toward the sunrising. And they answered Joshua, saying, All that thou commandest us we will do, and whithersoever thou sendest us, we will go. According as we hearkened unto Moses in all things, so will we hearken unto thee: only the LORD thy God be with thee, as he was with Moses. Whosoever he be that doth rebel against thy commandment and will not hearken unto thy words in all that thou commandest him, he shall be put to death: only be strong and of a good courage." ~ **Joshua chapter 1**

This is a passage of scripture few civilians have read, been drawn to, or heard preached. Here is a change of command, passing power and authority to another favored by God because of his God-like faith. God gives awesome power and authority to his chosen ones. Do you consider yourself chosen?

"Behold I give unto <u>you</u> power to tread on serpents and scorpions and over all the <u>power</u> of the enemy, and nothing by any means shall hurt <u>you</u>." ~**Luke 10:19**

If you believe he is speaking to <u>you</u>. Do you wield the power offered in this verse? We see from scripture both Moses and Joshua had a special, intimate relationship with God. Can you grab hold of divine promises? They did. Many are offered to us throughout the Bible. This ability certainly depends on your relationship with God. Most seem to choose to distance themselves from God. Do not come too close,

God! When we are faced with defeat and despair and need a breakthrough, don't we wish our relationship was closer? We need to purposefully decide to draw closer before any crisis occurs. When the crisis comes, it is too late.

Satan is out to steal, capture, and destroy. Have you felt his hot breath and raw power? If not, at some point, you will. Many believers seem to cower and run when the challenge to their delegated power and authority comes. Why? Satan fights to keep them from learning who they are "in Christ." I must admit earlier in life, after praying at some point in personal struggles, I gave up too quickly before God's breakthrough came. I have, at times, missed God's best for me by getting caught up in the emotion of the moment.

Millennials have been mostly trained up not to look to parents or God when in trouble but to call the experts in society. The policeman, lawyer, doctor, counselor, etc. They may try to "out nice" someone who is not nice and get mad to the point of crying when that does not work. Some want to call 911 for anything they cannot cope with and expect their needs to be met. This does not work well in a world gone mad. People are increasingly under the direct or indirect influence or control of demons. We need to be trained to call out for divine help first and expect God to respond. He can show up before any 911 help arrives in these days of the Antifa and BLM riots.

in combat

In combat, when someone shoots at you, you are trained to shoot back if that is what the rules of engagement permit. Our society, as it grows colder toward Christ, is increasingly combative. Civilians are trained to ask for professional help no matter the response time. When things really breakdown, as in CHOP in Seattle, a local business could expect no response from the police. Millennials are at an increasing disadvantage because of such breakdowns. They are not trained up to fight or figure it out even in a noncombative manner. Very frankly, the majority of younger

Americans have no real understanding of how to respond physically or spiritually when tested outside the box of their comfort zone. Increasing numbers never think about a spiritual response. In short, everyone needs frequent spiritual combat training. But few will ever get it outside of their own effort to pursue such knowledge as is in this book. Acting like victims does no help.

"The thief cometh not, but for to steal, and to kill, *and to destroy...." ~ **John 10:10***

The devil fights using people that do not fight fairly. That is why carnal Christians are at such a disadvantage in these end times. Carnal means worldly.

*"We are more than conquerors in Christ Jesus who loves us." ~**Romans 8:37***

conscripted

The Bible is clear: we who truly believe have been conscripted (enlisted into the army of God). We must learn to fight under godly authority with godly weapons. This is the only way we will prevail and overcome the breakdown in society only increasing. Everyone who is not born again, is still inside the enemy camp. That camp occupies most of the world. Those in that camp may be very nice people most of the time. They may seem innocent. But deceived they are. When the chips are down they are not reliable. Maybe even evil! We are all born behind enemy lines. Even if we are not part of Satan's active army, many are more comfortable in Satan's world than among Spirit-filled people. The only way to come out of the world is to surrender one's life to the living God. He will then help us come out more completely. All around us, we see people more or less under the influence of Satan.

We see many believers who are weak-willed, anemic, troubled, and conflicted. They seem to have little or no will to fight. They certainly would not be much help to anyone in a real fight. Deception is everywhere. Where are the overcomers who understand the authority they have been given in Christ? Those who know the power of His Name and the power of His Word? Those who operate in real authority!

We see a few with a biblical world view who are standing with God. But in close around us, more than likely, we feel much of the time all alone spiritually. Most people really do not have someone they know well they can really talk with or rely on in a time of trouble. Who do you know that can pray a prayer that will really make a difference in your life? Those who are the seed of Satan should fear us. That is if we truly understand and operate in the power of God! We need not fear them. We clearly have been given more power than they have been given by Satan.

"Ye are of God, little children, and have overcome them: because greater is he that is in you than he that is in the world." ~ **I John 4:4**

How do we develop the faith of an overcomer? We must believe in the finished work of Jesus Christ; that he is at the top of our various earthly chains of command. There is no other way to reach the necessary level of faith but by humbling one's self and surrendering to the True God. Compared to Jesus, we are all just his humble soldiers. Then we must seriously begin studying God's Word as if it was a life-or-death matter. We must drill it into our mind, will, and emotions.

We must become a disciple. A disciplined one! This is a step up from mere belief as a Christian. We certainly are not there if we still think of ourselves as just a member of some particular Christian denomination or group. For years I thought of myself as a Catholic. Not as a believer! We must look to Heaven where our Father dwells. We must see Jesus as our elder brother and LORD. The Holy Ghost should be our best friend. What a divine helper! This is not often the

48

case for those raised inside the church until they become born again. Only real surrender changes our position with Christ. He alone is the head of the army of God. To be in his chain of command, we must be out from under the devil's authority and power. We should look to no human as an intermediary between Christ and us.

So many that are raised inside the church think they are born again when they are not. I was one of those! But I had never had a transforming experience. One I was excited to share with others! Having no real testimony, I lacked the boldness to share my faith: one very important clue as to who is born again and who is not. I cannot say I was an ambassador of Christ. I had never seen a miracle, healing, or deliverance that my mind did not explain away as chance or just a wonderful coincidence. Religious zeal can masquerade as boldness, but there is a difference. I cannot say I really had a boldness that counts before my surrender. To really understand authority is to begin to walk in it. To know God's heart in a circumstance! To feel the anointing to do God's will in a particular situation! That knowledge transforms one's thinking. Do not go on to the next chapter without answering the below questions. Know for sure that you understand real authority and where you are in the chain of command.

Once again, real spiritual authority begins with a final surrender. You must put yourself in the grave with Christ by dying to yourself before you will truly begin to grasp the power of the resurrected life. It means He is in you, and you are in Him. If you are fearful and lack such boldness, then hang around the scriptures having to do with authority in the Bible, all 46 of them, until you have an epiphany. A paradigm shift in understanding! A deep download from heaven of new revelations!

You need to understand the importance of the chains of command you are in, and how demons can hinder their effectiveness. Besides the obvious words in this important phrase, words like a king (2386 uses), power (281), authority (46), and seat (312, meaning position) are key. Of course, there are other important words like dominion we could discuss when discussing this topic. Also, responsibility and accountability, etc. But I want to limit chapter sizes.

chain of authority

Look at the word *"Chain"* in the chapter title. It has 47 uses in the King James Bible that I use. The first use is **Genesis 41:42-43** *"And Pharaoh took off his ring from his hand, and put it upon Joseph's hand, and arrayed him in vestures of fine linen, and put a gold <u>chain</u> about his neck...."* For the sake of time, I did not write out verse 43, which is very important to read to see this bestowing of power and authority on this former slave and prisoner: the only one who could interpret Pharaoh's dreams. Pharaoh made him second in the chain of command of Egypt. Talk about a promotion! He saved the kingdom and his family during the hard times of famine with the divine help of God. But for years it didn't seem God took notice of him at all.

Look at the second important word in the phrase *"Chain of Command." "Command"* is used 554 times in the KJB. Wow! Believers who have little to no power to overcome in the battles,we are in are more likely to just ask, hope, or even beg than to command. But the LORD of Hosts in His Holy Word calls us who believe, *priests and kings.* Does He not? I cannot take the time to go through all 554 uses, though I would like to. If I did, I would lose most readers. For the sake of brevity, I will pick just a few verses to make my point.

Genesis 2:16 "And the LORD God <u>commanded</u> the man, saying Of every tree of the garden thou mayest freely eat: But of the tree of the knowledge of good and evil, thou shalt not eat of it: for in the day that thou eatest thereof thou shalt surely die."

Comment: Look what man feeds on today. We are still eating from this tree and dying spiritually like flies with physical death following close behind. It is rare today for men to feed more from the tree of life, the Word of God, which is sharper than any two-edged sword. A few men, for instance, Smith Wigglesworth, did and became mighty men of God. I encourage readers to really dig in. To study and meditate on the verses, God draws them to study! If we really want to get a hold of how to fight in the realm of the spirit world where the war is raging, influencing the outcome in the natural world, we will not learn how in the classrooms or assigned texts at secular universities or by feeding from MSN. I will skip for the sake of time over many interesting verses to:

Psalms 7:6 *"Arise, O LORD, in thine anger, lift up thyself because of the rage of mine enemies: and awake for me to the judgment that thou hast <u>commanded</u>."*

Comment: Did you know God has already commanded judgment against your enemies? But just like David of old, you may need to remind him of this fine point. Like with David, he will defend us too; if we will humble ourselves and cry out like David did. God listens to what we say. He sees our unbelief, doubt, and worry as well as our needs. They so often short circuit what he intends for us, for he will not go against our expressed will. How important it is to understand God's Word! His chain of command! We must apply it to our particular situation in the Mighty Name of Jesus Christ as we pray in earnest to our Heavenly Father.

Matthew 4:3-4 *"And when the tempter came to him, he said, If thou be the Son of God, <u>command</u> that these stones be made bread. But he answered and said, It is written, Man shall not live by bread alone, but by every word that proceedeth out of the mouth of God."*

Comment: Here, we see that Satan understood how powerful the use of God's own words are in changing our natural circumstance when life turns against us. Jesus counters with another scripture to offset what Satan is trying to trick him into doing. Satan, through his demons, tries to trick us too. We more than likely fall into his traps periodically because we don't feed daily on his written word. Waiting on him for a rhema word from heaven is good too in overcoming a particularly frustrating situation.

I Corinthians 7: 10-17 "*And unto the married, I* command *yet not I but the Lord, Let not the wife depart from her husband....*"

Comment: There is much confusion and bad teaching out there about marriage, divorce, and remarriage due to misunderstandings and false teachings. Much confusion and shame would go away among the believing community if believers living in doubt and sin would read and comprehend what Jesus teaches in chapter seven instead of looking to human teachers. I will finish u up with the last use of command in the Bible:

Revelation 9:4 "*And it was* commanded *them that they should not hurt the grass of the earth, neither any green thing, neither any tree; but only those men which have not the seal of God in their foreheads.*"

Comment: This is during the Great Tribulation. God's wrath is being poured out. He is in command. Satan is not. God is. The born-again believers have been raptured off the earth. God is dealing in his mercy with those who have been stubborn and rebellious, wishing that none would be lost. If a believer is to overcome in such trying times, he must understand the importance of commanding versus asking or begging or hoping. He must understand who is above him in the chain of command. Or if he is even in God's chain of command! Such an understanding is critical to what happens to him and others he loves and cares about. I do not think the gravity of the situation will be understood during this scary and terrifying period. One who doesn't take the time to read through many more of these important uses of just this one word *"command will not likely survive long."*

in closing

So, in closing, where does a person who has enlisted in the army learn about authority and power? It starts in boot camp! First, he reports for duty. Second, you quickly learn you know nothing. Third, you are disciplined during every moment of the day and night, when you are eating, sleeping, exercising, and training. Fourth, you begin to gain confidence by learning and doing. At the close of this experience, you graduate and are sent to another school as a graduate for more learning and training and eventually are assigned to a functioning unit of well-trained soldiers. It is similar in the spiritual world. There are pastors, teachers, prophets, evangelists, and apostles who God works through to equip the saints for the work of the ministry. We see that Jesus chose the twelve, and then they followed him everywhere, watching him teach and heal and deliver. Finally, he anointed them with authority and power and sent them out two and two. First the twelve, then the seventy, and finally the 120. When they were trained and ready, he commissioned them and went back to heaven. But not before destroying all the power of the enemy at the "cross' through his death, burial, and resurrection. Putting the enemy to flight. And he has told us this:

"Verily, verily, I say unto you, He that believeth on me, the works that I do shall he do also; and greater works than these shall he do; because I go unto my Father. And whatsoever ye shall ask in my name that will I do, that the Father may be glorified in the Son. If ye shall ask any thing in my name, I will do it."
*~ **John 14:12-14***

4

DRILL AND TRAINING

Most who enlist in the armed forces have colorful memories of their boot camp days. This experience for me occurred in 1961, a year before I graduated from college. I was in an officer training program (NROTC) and was a Marine option student, so I was sent to Quantico, Virginia. A very tough boot camp! There were 47 candidates in my platoon. Six weeks later, we had been whittled down to 27 who graduated this intense voluntary training. Why so difficult?

Because the successful ones would be commanding future Marines, possibly in Cuba, the current hot spot the summer of 1961! As I write this thought it is hard to believe that it was 60 years ago. It was a hot, sweaty summer full of drill, marches, exercise, overnight training, stuffy classroom presentations, and general harassment. This was in addition to what I experienced once a week while in college as an ROTC student on a much smaller scale. Everything the enlisted

Marine goes through in boot camp, plus... That was not all. A year later, upon graduation from college and commissioning, there was more of all this in more detail for six months at the Basic Officer Course at Quantico. Also, an unforgettable life experience! The rich history that is taught there, and for Christians, the Bible too is full of heroic stories.

There is another word for drill, the word *memorize*. This English word is not in the KJV Bible. Neither is the English word, rapture. That does not mean such concepts are not important. Just hidden using other words. When you investigate, you will be surprised to discover much of importance you have never heard preached from the pulpit. Look for synonyms.

Does it not seem this passage below is telling us to memorize (drill in) the written word of God?

"And these words, which I command thee this day, shall be in thine heart: And thou shall teach them diligently unto thy children, and shalt talk of them when thou sittest in thine house, and when thou walkest by the way, and when thou liest down, and when thou risest up. And thou shalt bind them for a sign upon thine hand, and they shall be as frontlets between thine eyes. And thou shalt write them upon the posts of thy house., and on thy gates." ~*Deuteronomy 6: 6-9*

conquering giants

If you read the previous five verses and those following (the context for the quote above), you see these Old Testament believers needed God's prior spoken words to prevail when they entered the battle with the giants in the land of promise. Without such drilling, you will never cross your Jordan or conquer the real giants in your life. They had to fight and conquer their giants physically to receive what was given to them. It is not much different for us today.

We, too, have giants to conquer. The demons that plague us today are often the negative giants in our minds (such as rejections, taunts, belittlements, false accusations, rages, profanities, depressions, separations, divorces, firings, fears, worries, etc.). These challenges are a part of life. The wise will learn to weld God's power effectively against these *"fiery darts of the enemy." These mental and emotional challenges can* take us out just as effectively as any visible arrow (bullet) fired by an enemy. We must learn to fight spiritually, or we will be taken out physically.

Many Christians I know are hard-pressed to quote a single verse from God's Holy Bible that can save them when mental anguish is threatening to overcome them. When these attacks come, one does not have the time to jump into the believer's warfighting guide to find out how to achieve victory.

Without such knowledge, how can we overcome the many giants we face in this generation: attacks (despair, suicidal thoughts, worries, doubts, unbelief, possible failures, alcohol or drug urges, pornography addictions) and in your face actual physical actions against you must be met with confidence and force at the moment of attack.

Let me mention the day I was sworn in as a second lieutenant of Marines at my university graduation. It was in August during the summer of the World Fair in Seattle. My proud parents were there. Also, a future wife. It was a warm summer day. Such an exciting day! Even though I was in great shape physically and had a degree academically; and had head knowledge about being a Marine, I was not yet fit to weld the authority and power vested in me that day in that swearing in ceremony. I now had the title: officer of Marines. But no office of yet! And more training was just ahead. There were many things I needed to drill into my mind, will and emotions to gain the competence that is needed for such an office. No one yet would be placed under my command. Yet war was on the horizon, and if a grave enough threat came I very likely could have been thrown into the breech. The Cold War was threatening to become very real. The Cuban Missile Crisis loomed big in everyone's mind. The news was of little else. This chapter emphasizes getting prepared ahead for what is coming.

As I prepared to write this morning, an interesting and timely news title popped up on my computer:

Newt Gingrich: A secret war is being fought all around us – And you may become a target
By Newt Gingrich | Fox News

The US is in a cyberwar
The war Newt wrote about is just one aspect of the spiritual war we are all engaged in. Maybe it hasn't yet become real enough to you. It involves hacking systems, spreading propaganda through social media, stealing identities, etc. We are fighting a new war, with an invisible front line and an indiscernible enemy. We can be attacked at any time without warning. Many internet users aren't doing enough to fortify and protect ourselves. It is not a visible war but is going on between nations. It is a behind the scenes war that includes cyber-attacks on civilian companies, governments, and intellectual property theft such as stealing military and civilian secrets.

My book is essentially about how to fight an invisible war and not get wounded or killed. But I thought this article was appropriate to mention. It seemed a confirmation to me I was in God's will with this book. A question: Are you prepared for this secret war Newt mentions? If you have a telephone, computer, television, or smart device, you should find it interesting.

Drill is all about preparation. Most work eight hours in a routine job. Then go home to family and friends, play and entertainment. There is, of course, homework if we are not to become obsolete. It can be hard work to stay up with progress and ahead of your peers.

learning vicariously

It was in the third year after commissioning that I entered a combat zone for the first of my three tours: all in Vietnam. When you are assigned to an infantry regiment, battalion, rifle company, or platoon, the secondary mission is always training. The drill is a great technique to iron in the automatic responses needed in a firefight. How to use your equipment, how to communicate quickly and efficiently, how to conduct various operations successfully requires a drill. Practice makes perfect is an old saying. And professional military schooling comes along as one progresses in a career.

I entered a combat zone for the first time in early December 1964 as a combat observer. The war raged for South Vietnam's Marines. Eighteen of us from SSgt to Captain were sent from various units in Hawaii and Okinawa to observe Vietnamese Marine fighting units for thirty days, close up. Our mission was to watch what they did in actual operations against the enemy and inform our units upon our return. To be the sole American among Asians was a unique experience for me. Marines are the same everywhere. I had met a few Vietnamese officers at the Basic School while there. This was different. Actual combat! In those 30 days, several of the observers experienced fierce combat and were overrun. One observer and a Vietnamese Marine escaped and evaded for half a month before reaching safety.

Another Marine won the Silver Star by taking charge when Vietnamese leaders were killed. The senior Marine, in our observation group, a Captain, was wounded and captured. He spent seven years in captivity and ended up dying after three attempted escapes. A U.S. Navy destroyer was named after him. These were serious times. This happened to a small group of Americans, and more, before any of us knew officially we would be committed to this war that following spring.

fear a motivator but to what end

It is said that the *"fear of the LORD is the beginning of all wisdom."* I have heard this is the most frequent phrase in the Bible. If you never have the direct experience of soldiering, and most millennials won't, why should a millennial read this book? There is a remote chance they could be conscripted if war came to America. Yet we all get attacked frequently, but because it is spiritual, we might not see it correctly. Researchers say millennials are less interested in religious matters than those in prior generations. So, they are less likely to be aware of their needs. Sadly, most won't read this book or the Bible. This is too bad for them and our nation! Those who grow up in Christianity at least have some classroom head knowledge to fall back on. It is a startling experience for an individual to suddenly realize the spiritual world that was unseen to him is now more real than what he was seeing and hearing. Hopefully, such an awakening won't be for the first time at the moment of death. We hear of near-death experiences. God, in His mercy, is trying to wake up those not yet hardened against the gospel. Most of us will not encounter spiritual reality just at death, but so many go through life in a thick spiritual fog with no real spiritual understanding. All of us experience the occasional scare…but then settle back into spiritual blindness. It's what we know. I later tell the story of a marine officer who panicked that I had to relieve. He went through all the training but never drilled it into his heart and was found wanting at the point of personal danger.

worth fighting for

Walking with young Vietnamese marines in the jungle during that month as an observer and going on their combat operations, I strangely never felt fear. On one operation, we attacked a trapped Viet Cong battalion. In a panic, they attacked over a blocking force, a dug-in ARVN battalion that had chased them onto that narrow bit of land surrounded on three sides by water. We assaulted off landing craft onto that peninsula. To get out of the way of our frontal assault (such was their fear of these marines), they attacked over the blocking force and escaped. Such was their fear of the Vietnamese Marines. My training in boot camp had built this absence of fear into me.

Because of my combat training back in the states, I strangely felt no fear. It might also have been because I had a certain level of awareness of God's protection. I was a practicing Roman Catholic. It was a strange time for me in many ways. No one spoke English except one officer that had been to schooling at Quantico. He was busy doing his job, usually elsewhere. All I could do was watch and observe. This regiment of Marines was led mostly by men from the north. All the leaders were Catholics who had fled communism. Intimately they knew what they were fighting against. They would have been executed if captured. These men were Marines. Maybe half were Catholics, and half were Buddhists. Like all Marines worldwide, they acted like bold lions when necessary. As much as is possible, their enemies seemed to avoid contact while I was with them. Their foes only fought when their backs were up against a wall. We moved a lot during those 30 days. Fortunately for me, the main fighting was elsewhere. Other observers seemed to experience more fighting than we did.

This short experience as a stranger among strangers was unique. Only two of us from the regiment in Hawaii were chosen. It occurred over Christmas and the New Year celebrations. It was offered to several others more senior before being offered to me. Maybe I was too stupid and naive to understand the danger I would be exposed to. That faraway war was not on my mind for sure—just an occasional story on the news. I had no inkling our unit would soon be deployed to that hot spot. But if it happened, I thought this experience would give me a better chance of surviving a 13-month combat tour if it came to that. It was a wake-up call for me. My family was looked after as my mother-in-law came over to help my wife during my absence.

civilians can profit from a soldier's perspective

Many times, you have to repeat the truth often until it becomes real to you. One truth not preached well by pastors is that we all live in a spiritual combat zone. Conventional wisdom won't teach this. Children are raised up not knowing many of the dangers to their bodies and souls. Most are never taught how to fight spiritually. Let the professionals fight for you. Of course, nothing of the spiritual dangers that abound! Or that there is continued existence after death for your soul.

That what you see, hear, touch, smell, and taste is not the sum of life. That demons are actually real, not just figments of one's imagination. There is no such thing as heaven or hell. There is no Creator. Evolution is fact, not theory. Prayers are not important to life outcomes. In fact: most of us are raised to believe multiple lies. There is little understanding of true reality for multitudes. Combat soldiers have faced death, have stories to tell if civilians cared to listen and that is the root of most P.T.S.D. episodes.

few military recruits understand this truth

"Be sober, be vigilant; because your adversary the devil, as a roaring lion walketh about seeking whom he may devour:" ~ *I Peter 5:8*

Military chaplains were first appointed to serve during the War of Independence in 1776. Congress at the beginning of this war, understood the importance of putting Bibles in the hands of soldiers. Our chaplaincy back then was solely Christian up through WWII. During America's war for independence, spiritual help was not complicated by teachings from other religious world views like Islam. This is no longer true. A real understanding of eternity no longer fortifies the thinking of most younger Americans. Teaching scriptural truths has no meaning for many in this Millennial generation. They have been inoculated against Bible teachings by the secularists who control American education.

One of the chaplain's duties is to be sure men repent of their sins, forgive those who have offended them, and are certain of who their savior is before going into intense fighting where they might be killed. Chaplains try to be close at hand where men are being wounded and dying, to help them spiritually in such tense moments. That is their real job. But in truth, today, you can enlist for four years' service and after discharge can't remember ever meeting or hearing a chaplain speak, except maybe occasionally at a Sunday service, if motivated to attend.

Disease, accidents, murders, and such claim a lot of souls. These have no relationship to most actual wartime experiences. When stacked up against actual combat deaths, Satan probably claims far more souls for his kingdom from deaths not related to actual combat. Aftermath of wars can be hell for veterans without spiritual help.

To be truthful, we are not now in 2021, far from the coming horrors talked about in the Book of Revelation. Yet, most Christians have never read this book or heard a sermon preached from it. The four horsemen of the Apocalypse are now riding across the earth. We are in the long prophesized *"birth pangs."* During the Great Tribulation, most of the armies of the world will end up in the Valley of Meggido under the control of Satan and his antichrist. Military boot camps will be busy before this prophesied time. You do not want to be there for that gruesome slaughter. If you are going to enlist in the military out of financial necessity, or if God is calling you into this mission field, then before you go off to boot camp, invest some time in the Bible to determine if you are even saved.

Military chaplains today, if they know the truth, are now hamstrung administratively by political correctness with respect to sharing many biblical truths. Bottom line: there are death angels out to kill and maim. As protected and trained as you might think you are from the standpoint of the natural realm, you need to also understand how to protect yourself supernaturally.

Look at the policy and procedure manuals of the secular institutions today across America. You will not find many offering any supernatural perspective at all. Satan is the great deceiver. Sadly, he has blinded the secular teachers and instructors concerning any understanding of spiritual warfare. If you have a godly grandmother or parent, you may have picked up some spiritual warfare training. But such grandparents and parents are increasingly rare. (**Amos 8:11 II Timothy 3**)

armor of God

Your mom or grandmother might have talked to you about the armor of God. You may even have read this critical passage in **Ephesians 6: 11-18:**

"Put on the whole armor of God, that ye may be able to stand against the wiles of the devil. For we wrestle not against flesh and blood, but against principalities, against powers, against the rulers of this world, against spiritual wickedness in high places. Wherefore take unto you the whole armor of God, that ye may be able to withstand in the evil day, and having done all, to stand. Stand therefore, having your loins girt about with truth, and having on the breastplate of righteousness; and your feet shod with the preparation of the gospel of peace; Above all, taking the shield of faith, wherewith ye shall be able to quench all the fiery darts of the wicked. And take the helmet of salvation, and the sword of the Spirit, which is the word of God: Praying always with all prayer and supplication in the Spirit, and watching thereunto with all perseverance and supplication for all saints,"

These are not idle words. They address your actual supernatural protection offered by God himself. I try to declare them every morning in the shower. Have you developed the habit of doing so? It distinguishes mature believers from everyone else.

If a believer is to overcome in this Age of Grace that is quickly coming to a close, he needs to really meditate on, and believe there is, divine power available to us. And then fight evil in a scriptural manner in the way this entire passage indicates for:

"We wrestle not against flesh and blood, but against principalities, against powers, against the rulers of the darkness of this world, against spiritual wickedness in high places. Wherefore take unto you the whole armour of God, that ye may be able to withstand in the evil day, and having done all, to stand." ~ ***Ephesians 6:12-13***

When I was a student lieutenant at the Basic School (1962-63), each of us was given a small booklet loaded with short combat stories, good warfare history, and solid wisdom. I remember one story from WWI very well. There was this staff officer who would come down and meet with soldiers fresh off the battlefield. Many shell shocked because of the carnage witnessed. He would encourage them. One of the things he told to increase their morale and esprit de corps was this story.

A British captain commanding an infantry rifle company was in a regiment assigned to the frontlines against the Germans. He had his men get together by twos each morning and declare **Psalm 91** out loud in prayer. He had them memorize these sixteen verses.

"He that dwelleth in the secret place of the most high shall abide under the shadow of the Almighty. I will say of the LORD. He is my refuge and my fortress: my God; in him will I trust. Surely he shall deliver thee from the snare of the fowler, and from the noisome pestilence. He shall cover thee with his feathers, and under his wings shall thou trust: his truth shall be thy shield and buckler. Thou shalt not be afraid for the terror by night nor for the arrow that flieth by day: Nor for the pestilence that walketh in darkness; nor for the destruction that wasteth at noonday. A thousand shall fall at

thy side, and ten thousand at thy right hand; but it shall not come nigh thee. Only with thine eyes shall thou behold and see the reward of the wicked. Because thou hast made the LORD, which is my refuge, even the most High, thy habitation; There shall no evil befall thee, neither shall any plague come nigh thy dwelling. For he shall give his angels charge over thee, to keep thee in all thy ways. They shall bear thee up in their hands, lest thou dash thy foot against a stone. Thou shalt tread upon the lion and adder: the young lion and the dragon shalt thou trample under feet. Because he hath set his love upon me, therefore will I deliver him: I will set him on high, because he hath know my name. He shall call upon me, and I will answer him: I will be with him in trouble, I will deliver him, and honor him. With long life will I satisfy him and show him my salvation."

In the horrible fighting this infantry company experienced, they had fewer casualties than any other company. That regiment had over 50% killed, if I recall correctly. Trench warfare was awful!

My question: Have you set your love upon him? Are you drilling in the written word of God? What wonderful protection if you have. Do you understand you are under divine authority and have been given authority and power of your own in his spiritual chain of command? Are these passages above worth memorizing? Drilling into your whole being? For those who want these divine promises in Psalm 91 to be theirs it is the only way.

Our world is full of troubles and sorrows, but for those who have experienced God in a real way, he is with us always and there to bring us through to victory. If you think in this book that I am spending too much time on the problems, then read a bit further because I will always provide a way through the problems. There is always a path through for those who have the will to overcome.

5

A DISCIPLE'S DISCIPLINE

Much has been written about the importance of discipline. The bigger the challenge, the more "self-denial" is an essential ingredient for success. And self means self. All of us experience external discipline in this life for the sake of the general welfare. But it is our own disciplining of self that sets one apart from the majority. In the last chapter, I ended with quotes from two passages. I challenged readers to spend time in these passages. Doing so takes time and focus. Not many are motivated to iron in such supernatural protection sources (scripture verses) before a major attack comes, but then it is too late. Good habits need to become second nature. That takes time. Such a personal effort can transform us in meaningful ways. But the distractions that divert us from these important efforts are many and much more fun. Discipline provides strength in the time of need, a cool head, and the self-control needed to overcome the challenge.

What can I add to the many conversations about and the teachings one has heard and experienced on the need for individual discipline? Think back on all the teachers over your life, beginning with your mother; all that advice given. Maybe you never spent quality time with a warfighter and committed believer among them. Well, now maybe is the time to absorb the lessons in this book. Seeing things from a different angle can be extremely helpful. I hope to trigger additional fight in you to overcome personal issues that have held you back. What are you struggling with or putting off that needs doing? In my lifetime, I have noticed many give up the struggle to overcome and wonder why. Others seem to have no fight in them almost from birth. Has a bad habit like smoking finally defeated you? Do you always cave to a significant other who does not have your best interest in mind?

Real trouble comes when a stubborn person burns through the last family member who really cares. Now there is no one else motivated enough to step in and help. Our flesh is very rebellious. It resists family help. Those who alienate their own family are legends. Of course, there are professionals who get paid to help others. But such help is costly and mostly nonpersonal. And most Christian professionals must put aside their spiritual understanding because they are restrained by the organization's concern about the threat of lawsuits from the atheists. I have seen people get solid advice from complete strangers (out of the blue) that is often also rejected. And there is a definite lack of appreciation where such help is given free by the good-hearted. Ungratefulness is widespread in our society today. Even among believers!

inner strength

If a person always looks to others for help lacking personal resources because of laziness, they are eventually forced to go it alone. Lack of inner strength is a definite problem for many. When one is in the habit when trouble comes of looking to others for help; having never prepared for emergencies themselves; then that help may not be available, and they must reap what they have sown by their lack of personal discipline. Too many people seldom or never look to God at such times. And he is the source of all supernatural help.

Developing self-discipline is tough. It requires the inner strength to sacrifice personally for some greater outcome. Most civilian organizations do not offer the external discipline that military units do out of necessity. So, a soldier is apt to learn the importance of self-discipline more quickly than a civilian. But so few Americans will ever join the military voluntarily. Of course, if war comes upon us, then we must resort to involuntarily enlisting citizens for the good of the nation, and the training they get will profit them when they are released from active duty. I have asked God to put an anointing on this book to draw such people. We all need to understand the importance of divine help. This knowledge is not available in most books and texts written today. There is a growing famine of the Word of God.

There are many writings by men with more actual time in combat than I experienced. They will likely sell more copies. But they will not offer any real spiritual understanding. I have thumbed through many such books and novels. People must be inspired by God to ever pick up a good spiritual read. The world hates such books. And Satan works hard to keep people out of them just as he does the Bible: which is the greatest of all warfighter primers. It is the main source I draw my inspiration from. According to Jesus Christ, Satan is the ruler over mankind until he returns as promised to restore order on planet earth. (**Revelation 19:11-16**) He will, in due season, take the earth back from the grip of the Evil One.

muscle strength

I think back over the many times I pushed my muscles to gain strength and speed for the sports I desired to excel in. I think too of the temporary suffering that came

69

from strenuous exercise. Staying in shape to pass the yearly Marine Corps fitness tests with a good score required time and effort. It was an important task to set a proper example for those younger in one's command. That physical and mental discipline helps establish patterns in life that lead to the great health I now experience over my 82 years of life. Sharpening one's scriptural knowledge by private personal study does not happen just by sitting every Sunday under academic teaching from a pastor. Looking back over a lifetime of Sunday teachings, I must say that most impacted me more like a lecture than a one-on-one encounter. Of lectures, it has been said that *"the notes of the teacher pass to the notes of the students without going through the minds of either."*

The talented wicked also know a need for discipline

I am astounded that the end for most of the rich and famous does not end well. From reading obituaries, I see that many suffer much in their later years. I wonder how many ever get right in their old age before they die. Often, I find no indication of salvation. It is all about their great accomplishments while alive. To die and wake up in eternity, not knowing the Living God? Terrifying! What a shock for them.

It takes discipline even to be a successful, well-respected crook. You must be careful to camouflage your secret life so that you will not end up in jail where you belong. Evil people must work hard to stay out of jail. To be wicked and live a long life and end up in hell? How is that possible without a considerable degree of self-discipline? The majority of people aren't successful in this life. Why is that? They cannot seem to discipline themselves sufficiently to keep from having problems eventually overwhelm them.

One strong reason for external discipline is so that society will have a certain modicum of order. Bringing about the order so that the unruly are kept from harassing most people is what the police, investigators, judges, and prison officials are commissioned to do. They keep the worst of the undisciplined troublemakers in line so the rest of us can live peaceful lives. Look at how many parking tickets and speeding tickets the city police give out daily to otherwise law-abiding citizens. Many are responsible, hardworking adults and almost never make trouble for others. The lawbreakers always have their eyes out for signs of police activity. Many by such discipline avoid being caught to what final benefit? Providing the necessary external discipline to keep the undisciplined from troubling the lives of the more productive is an important police duty.

out of control emotions

The Bible exhorts us to:

"Study to show thyself approved unto God, a workman that need not be ashamed, rightly dividing the word of truth." ~II Timothy 2:15

Nightly in the news, we see various people make the news by not controlling their emotions. Road rage incidents are one example. I like to think I am a good driver and a courteous one, but I confess I have "set someone off" who did not like something I did while driving. Now it is hard to apologize when driving down the road because you made a mistake. But an apology probably wouldn't be accepted anyway by many today. It seems a growing number of citizens look for things to be angry about. Have you noticed this trend? There is increasingly less patience for those who do not measure up to the standards of "the hotheads." Pulling out a gun and shooting someone who offends them is more common every day in places like Chicago. What's with that! Places across America are unraveling before our very eyes. Controlling one's emotions is critical in everyday life. A growing number cannot even do this. It shows we are sliding toward the end of days more quickly every day.

Keeping myself in shape has been a top priority much of my life. The time spent playing sports and exercising when younger required self-discipline for sure if you wanted to be better than average. Looking back now, some of that time spent could have been more wisely used by me in light of the verse above's wisdom. Scripture tells us exercise is of little (or some) value. Studying about spiritual warfare (offense and defense) and disciplining one's self by drilling scripture into one's nature is certainly more valuable than time spent on physical and intellectual skill in light of the growing evil throughout society we are seeing in places like Portland. We actually have to believe in God and his willingness to reward the faithful to receive the promises of the Bible in our own lives.

"But without faith it is impossible to please him: for he that cometh to God must believe that he is, and that he is a rewarder of them that diligently seek him." ~**Hebrews 11:6**

A "hot head" who is triggered by raging anger can do a lot of damage. But there are far more evil people out there used by Satan in an indirect manner that does not draw public attention. We never become aware of most of them (Inventors of immunization cocktails laced with bad things, chemtrails that harm our crops and lungs, and those who put these wicked policies in place). Such people are far more creative in their evil deeds. How do we protect ourselves from these an;d take the fight to them spiritually?

It takes real discipline to pick up the Bible, study it, and then uses the weapons we find there against God's enemies. Even when we don't feel like studying, it makes sense to do so! At the start, when we decide to get our body into shape it is hard. Our flesh doesn't like being challenged. It's the same with our souls (mind, will, and emotions).

Most of us would rather be entertained than to study to show ourselves approved. Or if we like to study, maybe any secular topic is preferred ahead of learning what God has to say about a subject in his written word.

biorhythms

What are biorhythms? What does this have to do with self-discipline and spiritual warfare? The study of biorhythms helps us better understand ourselves and others. How it is that we sometimes "lose it."

Afterward we think, how could that have happened to me? That was not really like me to do or say such a thing. What was that trigger all about?

Biorhythms are recurring cycles in the physiology or functioning of a person. We see the daily cycle of sleeping and waking. Also, a cyclic pattern of the physical, emotional, or mental activity is said to occur in the life of a person.

This was an explanation from the internet., By typing in this word, charts pop up that show where you are on any given day. When you type in your birth date, you get a three-wave chart representing a 33-day long intellectual cycle, a 28-day long emotional cycle, and a 23-day long physical cycle. You can see what happened a few days before, what you are dealing with then, or what is coming up in the near future that your mind, body, or emotions will be dealing with. If you got triggered, you could check to see if it was on a critical day. It shows when you are positive, above the line, and when you are negative, below the line. The key time for you is the 24-hour period when you move across the line. It is a critical time. Things can happen that are not normal when you have a single, double, or triple critical day when your human nature is disturbed or troubled.Can you see the need for daily prayer?

Japanese airlines, I read years ago, warned their pilots on a single critical day but they could fly. On a double critical day, they could come to work but could not fly; and on a triple critical day, they were told to stay home. I also read that the Marine Corps did a study on drill Instructor incidents at boot camps involving recruits.

They found that most of the unfortunate incidents happened on double or triple critical days. I have also read that accidents and deaths are more likely to happen at such times. Good information? I think so!

But I don't rule my life by such charts. But it does motivate me to look to the living God who knows me better than I do and why I am motivated to pray frequently. Why is such knowledge important? No one should rule their lives by such charts. It is just another means of demonstrating the need for daily prayer and the importance of hearing from the Holy Spirit who can overcome our every weakness. Without His help, we are on our own. One more reason why we should develop the discipline of looking to God for divine help.

God helps his people

I know a woman who has the gift of perception. She is a perceiver. She was driving with her husband. I think it was in 2011. Maybe in June. Suddenly she was in a meeting somewhere else. When she came back into the car, this is what she told her husband: **"I went somewhere. I was suddenly in the corner of a room watching. There were twelve people in the room. Two were women. I recognized some of them. It was a room full of internationally important figures. At the head of the table, a man stood up with two sets of papers in his hand. He said: We are going to begin to poison the food supply. This is the list of food you can eat. This other list is the food you are to avoid. Then he sat down. And I then found myself back in the car with my husband still driving."** She then asked her husband, "Is there an international meeting going on somewhere?" He said, "Yes: The G-7 meeting in France."

Why do I tell you this? What does it have to do with discipline? There are things going on which you and I will never read about in any newspaper. There are things the elite, who think they run the world, do not want the majority to know. Like their war to reduce the population! The people would rise up and toss them out of power if they knew the truth. Most of us operate at some level of deception. Jesus tells us that Satan is the present ruler of this world. He controls directly or has indirect influence over the human systems of this world. Without divine dreams, visions, written prophecies, and direct words from God, his people would be blind to the actual evil going on.

*"And immediately, the Spirit driveth him into the wilderness." ~**Mark 1:12***

Here begins a fascinating story told by Jesus to his disciples about a direct encounter he had with the ruler of this world. Three times he was tempted and countered the temptation with the written Word of God. We are told here and elsewhere who is in charge of the world system. Satan! Yes, God is in control over him. That is why we need his divine help.

It takes personal discipline to change the pattern of our lives and stay under the influence of the Living Spirit of God. We must surrender our lives to another to get such help. No one can go through life alone, no matter how much he or she attempts to discipline himself. To overcome our own flesh and the supernatural evil God's word tells us is behind the world system; we must be born again and have access to God's authority and power. And then we must use it!

"Jesus answered and said unto him, Verily, verily I say unto thee, Except a man be born again, he cannot see the Kingdom of God...." ~ **John 3: 3, 6**

This is the famous night conversation Jesus had with Nicodemus, a leader of the Sanhedrin. Only those who are born again can begin to see the truth of what each of us contends against in this fallen world.

So, if what I reported above about this meeting of evil people really happened: widespread poisoning to reduce the world population is underway. How do we keep from being poisoned? First, we have to believe this story is true. Second, since we weren't given these two papers, we need to look to God and the power of his Word to stay in good health. No amount of exercise and good living will save us in these evil times in which we live. When Jesus sent out his disciples ahead of him, he told them *"to eat what was put in front of them."* This is still true today. So we must pray over our food and drink before we eat or drink. Also, we must believe what God says.

"And these signs shall follow those who believe.,..and if they drink (or eat) any deadly thing, it shall not hurt them..."~ **Mark 16: 17**

Of course, we also must listen to that still small voice and stay away from what we know naturally is harmful such as GMO foods; and eat healthy and organic when possible. But such things are not always possible. So, pray and trust God. And praise Him. And pray in the Spirit.

"He that speaketh in an unknown tongue edifieth himself."~*I Corinthians 14: 4*

By praying in the Spirit, we leave the particulars of the prayer to the Holy Spirit, who is our helper. If we have consumed poison through ChemTrails, poisoning of the food supplies (processed foods), or otherwise, the Spirit of God knows what to ask for and how to pray for us.

Such trust requires greater discipline than most exhibit. Such a walk is not a common one. Most believers do not study things out for themselves. Most of us are too trusting of men and women who have been placed over us in offices and positions. Most trust the government more than what the Bible tells them about life. Most because of television, movies, and what Goggle wants us to see on the internet, and doesn't make it difficult to find, are influenced by darkness and don't even know it. Many in leadership are not good people.

This book is more about spiritual warfare than natural warfare, which is also important in staying healthy and alive. What is going on in the spiritual realm (the war between Michael and God's angels and Satan and his fallen angels) greatly affects what we see and hear in the natural realm, including actual wars. When we enlist into a visible army like the U.S. Military, or after enlisting into God's army, which is invisible, we are likely and maybe unwittingly under the direct or indirect control of Satan. To a certain extent, we have all been programmed with upside-down thinking, false assumptions, and off base behaviors while in the world.

After being spiritually awakened, if we will start watching, we will see this upside-down thinking being acted out in society on the evening news.

"Woe unto them that call evil good, and good evil; that put darkness for light, and light for darkness; that put bitter for sweet, and sweet for bitter!"
~*Isaiah 5:20*

Do not stop with this one verse in Isaiah. Read the whole passage to get the impact of what God is telling us through this great prophet about the world system. It does not look out for our good in many cases.

It takes great discipline to walk in faith as a true believer. Why are so many who confess Christ and are good and decent people being overcome in this life rather than overcoming evil? It is because they do not study things out for themselves. They do not really trust God as much as they trust the so-called experts. Their trust is mostly in men. They operate in a mixture of belief and unbelief. I am sad when I say this because I am thinking of some I care about.

As a uniformed soldier, if you just depended on what you learned in classrooms and are made or told to do, you would not have as good a chance of survival. Those with a better chance are those who work hard to prepare themselves over and above what is required. Good soldiers don't just do the minimum required of them, do they?

"No man that wareth entangleth himself with the affairs of this life; that he may please him who hath chosen him to be a soldier." ~II Timothy 2:4

Our single focus should be to please God. This is hard to do. I am not there yet and have been working on it more diligently for the past 40 years. This book is as much for me as for you. I am striving towards the mark which Paul strived for.

"I press toward the mark for the prize of the high calling of God in Christ Jesus."
~Philippines 3: 14

It takes discipline to press forward in the face of opposition. Anything worth doing well will be opposed by someone. This reminds me of a story. In Vietnam on my third combat tour. A couple of months after being assigned to a rifle company as the commander, we were tasked with a short raid into the DMZ as a diversion. There was some kind of combined operation going on, and our forces were now being withdrawn. We were sent across the DMZ as a feigned reinforcement, as a diversion.

We were trucked to the northernmost NW combat outpost. I think its designation was A-1. It was manned by an ARVN battalion. There we rode out on twenty army tanks and ran into a dug-in North Vietnamese outfit that was freshly shaved and had just crossed the river dividing North from South Vietnam. One of our tanks came under fire off my left flank. I was told to attack the dug-in force trying to knock out that tank with an RPG. I so ordered the platoon commander on my left flank. Word came back through my gunnery sergeant that its commander was seized up with fear and not responsive. I rushed over to the area and led the rifle squad on that flank in a frontal assault against the dug-in enemy force.

They had a machine gun and an anti-tank weapon and were reinforced with artillery. With the support of the nearest tank's 50 calibers, we had no problem overrunning that position. The threat to the tank's crew ended.

I had to relieve the platoon commander. He had received the same training I had received at the Basic School. He had not been assigned an infantry officer M.O.S. He was a supply officer because of his extra schooling. But that situation overwhelmed him. It happens. He never thought he would ever be in an infantry situation and had not prepared himself mentally. He was reassigned to a rear area position. He had received all the infantry training I had but was not mentally tough. Our Division commander, General Ray Davis, had every rear officer assigned for 1-3 months as an infantry officer so they would be motivated to give his forward-deployed troops enthusiastic support. This lieutenant never thought he would come face to face with the enemy. And I believe that is the state of mind of many millennials today.

Scripture tells us a lot about fighting:

In **Jeremiah 48:10,** we learn this: *"Cursed is the man who refuses to fight."*

*In **II Corinthians 10: 3-4,** we read: "For the weapons of our warfare are not carnal, but mighty through God to the pulling down of strong holds; casting down imaginations, and every high thing that exalteth itself against* *the knowledge of God, and bringing into captivity every thought to the obedience of Christ..."*

People are often ambushed or triggered in this life. When it happens, they need a rehearsed response. That is what drill is all about. Will you be better prepared when Satan's next attack comes? That, in a nutshell, is what self-discipline is all about. When we come to the saving knowledge of Christ, **Romans 12** tells us we must:

*"... not be conformed to this world: but be ye transformed by the renewing of your mind, that ye may prove what is that good, and acceptable, and perfect, will of God." **Romans 12:1-2***

How do we accomplish this? The Bible tells us how:

*"For the weapons of our warfare are not carnal, but mighty through God to the pulling down of strong holds; Casting down imaginations, and every high thing that exalteth itself against the knowledge of God and bringing into captivity every thought to the obedience of Christ." ~***2 Corinthians 10: 3-4**

6

DIFFERENT TASKS

enlisting

The military branches of our armed forces need a continuous supply of new recruits. Our government counts on brave enough, patriotic men and women to enlist to keep us an all-voluntary military service force. Those who surrender their lives willingly for a period of service hopefully do so for the good of our nation. Volunteers make better fighters than those forced to enlist.

Before assigning particular skills (Military Occupational Specialties,) a recruit's capabilities and limitations are observed. They also are given written and practical tests to determine their aptitudes before being assigned a particular skill. Armies try to place people where they will do the most good. But the needs of the service do come first. So, some end up doing what wasn't their first or second choice. That is where prayer comes in. Many did not learn at the family level how to pray effectively or even how important it is to pray for favor in such circumstances.

This chapter's title suggests I might write about the many different tasks a military unit must accomplish when it fights another trained force while making comparisons with related spiritual warfare tasks. My approach will be a bit different. Armies must be fed. They run on their stomachs. Hungry soldiers do not fight well. This task alone is massive. It paints a stark picture of the great efforts devoted to preparing just the meals necessary for hungry soldiers in many different locations.

If truth is known, which most often it is not, a soldier, to enhance his survival odds, must also daily be feeding on God's Word too.

the great task

A spiritual army eats and drinks spiritual food. Jesus Christ is the Bread of Life. The Bible is food for starving souls. Believers, to gain strength, must feed on the Word of God. Hosea, the prophet, spoke for God when he said: *"My people perish for lack of knowledge."* This is what communion is about. Communion points to Jesus. Many believers are starving, and yet do not realize it. Their pastors are picking and choosing what to feed them from God's Word, not knowing their particular needs. Mostly it's a guess for them what to share on Sundays. Pastors, too, have their own biases. Pastors who do wait on the LORD and pray do hear from God, so of course, there will be more anointing on what they preach. We must blindly trust they will speak to our needs unless we too go to prayer and the Bible to influence what comes out of their mouths when they preach. How often do you pray for your pastor? Do you even have a pastor or trusted one?

Believers need supernatural energy from the Word to accomplish their assigned tasks properly. High morale is the first casualty to go when fighting units are not fed properly. God's army must be equipped properly to do its job. God appoints apostles, prophets, evangelists, teachers, and pastors

82

to train God's army. They must be Holy Ghost inspired to properly equip the saints. Yet I have wondered at times if the one preaching the message is even born again. Religious determination and zeal are not qualifications for office.

While many church leaders within the church system can academically talk about the Holy Ghost, the lack of power for healing and deliverance makes me wonder if the Holy Ghost is truly welcome in the midst of many gatherings. His presence is often not felt, and few leaders wait for him to show up in the service. We see from scripture that Jesus Christ was rejected at his first coming by many in the establishment. I wonder if, in the same way, the Holy Ghost is being rejected by many throughout Christendom as we approach the second coming of Christ. He is the Helper, and we need his help desperately as the anti-christ spirit grows noticeably stronger across the globe.

God gives each of us different giftings and skills. We all have talent that can be employed in the fight we are suppose to be engaged in. There is a fight to warn others of what is coming and of the reality of Jesus Christ. Satan wars against that Name, keeping many of us so bound up in fears, worries, doubts, and unbelief that many never join the fight against evil. So, the truth of the saving knowledge of Jesus Christ is a difficult truth to spread. Some believers even fear if they are even saved.

II Peter 1:10-11 exhorts us to make sure our calling and election is sure. Read this verse and take to heart this exhortation. How do we accomplish this if there is a battle going on in our minds telling us we are not even saved? We should not have a real hard time hanging on to the peace that passes all understanding. That peace is ours when we truly accept Christ as our savior. **Romans 10: 9-11** is meat to sustain us. Drill these three verses into your spirit until nothing, and no one can steal the joy of your salvation or stand between you and Christ.

"That if thou shalt confess with thy mouth the Lord Jesus, and shalt believe in thine heart that God hath raised him from the dead, thou shalt be saved. For with the heart man believeth unto righteousness; and with the mouth confession is made unto salvation. For the scripture saith, whosoever believeth on him shall not be ashamed."

households must be commanded

"For I know him, that <u>he will command his children and his household</u> after him, and they shall keep the way of the LORD, to do justice and judgment, that the LORD may bring upon Abraham that which he hath spoken of him."
~Genesis 18:19

The word <u>command</u> in the above verse above, is an important army term. Look at the word household or family in the Bible. We see household seventy times and family 228 times. If we go back far enough in the Bible, we see that to survive; families had to be able to fight and win. The constant threat of enemy assaults kept the Hebrews alert and sharp when they worshipped the only true God. Security was a primary task: as important as hunting, fishing, or farming was for survival.

In the Old Testament, we see living, life, and fighting were very physical. Our fight to overcome will be won or lost in the New Testament because of our spiritual decisions and gifting far more than our natural inclinations and abilities. We must learn about the authority and power given to us in the scriptures to prevail in the battles we most likely will face. At this age, the challenge for most is often more mental than physical. Despite the elite's attempts to blur distinctions between the sexes to create chaos to exploit, it is obvious to the wise that God made the sexes uniquely different. There should be no mental confusion on this point. It should be obvious from looking who God intended you to be. Regardless of how you feel at the moment. This is just one of many areas where right is becoming wrong and up, down, and evil, good and good, evil. This alone should tell you something is very wrong across America. You need God's help. Don't try to go it alone.

base attitudes

My wife loves to laugh, care for, and have fun with the family. Family is her primary focus outside of God. That is where her heart is. I, too, love our family. However, my focus is more outward beyond the home. The community, state, nation, and the world is where the real threat to my family lies. That is where my main focus as a man must be.

I do not think she and I are unique in this regard. These days the propaganda and training in our schools and media because of feminism and other ungodly cultural forces are increasingly the enemy of good. They are more and more under the influence of the evil one and are blurring the truth. There is much confusion and folly among the ranks of world leadership. Men and women are uniquely different. This is hard-wired (DNA) into our natures by God. Any deviations from this are clearly explained biblically despite raging hormones.

God does not make mistakes when he makes people. My wife's love of laughter is so healthy. I have come to notice over time that a healthy attitude more often than not results in a healthy body and mind. She is half Irish. Who laughs more than the Irish? By nature, I am more sober. Half English! The other two mixes in me, German, and French, don't seem to help me laugh often like my wife. She is especially important to me in keeping me balanced. She brings joy into my life. But I am soberly looking for ways to accomplish what I feel called by God to accomplish, such as this book.

I can put aside a relationship to accomplish an important task in a way she doesn't understand. She is rarely down. I am upbeat by nature myself. But some of the things

85

she sees on the humorous side are not funny to me. Why is this? Our basic natures are quite different. In one way, we are both the same. We are both born into this world with a sinful nature. Our capacity to sin means we both want our way. This does put us at odds at times.

"The heart is deceitful above all things and desperately wicked; who can know it?"
~ *Jeremiah 17: 9*

This verse is a comment about most decision-makers. God has made an allowance for the basic difference between the sexes. He established a chain of command at the family level. He has established men to be the head of families. Women are to be their husband's helpmates. Why are many who influence society working so hard to screw up this basic division of tasks at the family level and in society at large? Because Satan hates God's creation and order. He is trying to destroy it. Because so many humans are under his control and working for him and against God and his people; is one major reason life is becoming increasingly difficult. All humans are not made in the image of God. Proof?

"And I will put enmity between thee and the woman and between thy seed and her seed: it shall bruise thy head, and thou shalt bruise his heel." ~*Genesis 3:15*

This verse speaks strongly of two different seeds at war with each other. How is this possible?

"That the sons of God saw the daughters of men that they were fair; and they took them wives of all which they chose." ~*Genesis 6:2*

Who were the sons of God? Not men for sure but fallen angels.

"And the angels which kept not their first estate but left their own habitation, he hath reserved in everlasting

chains under darkness unto the judgment of the great day."
~Jude 1:6

Therefore the *"born again"* experience is so vital. God is the only one that can override our sin nature (corrupted DNA) by what he did for us at the cross. He died for us to make it possible for us to enter into heaven and overcome in this life. Each of us is a potential gift from God to others. We are created by Him for his pleasure and to be a blessing to others. But until we surrender our lives fully to God, we can drive others nuts. We are to see all through the eyes of God. As salvageable! But until they to surrender they remain under the influence of the enemy of our souls! This is very difficult to do. This is another major task: saving souls!

many tasks

There are so many different tasks to be accomplished in this world to make it run efficiently and effectively. But it is not our task to save the world. That is not the mission of a believer in Jesus Christ. Individual people are to be our focus. For most of us: one person at a time. Thank God we are all uniquely different. How do you see most people? As an obstacle to maneuver around? Or do you see their possibilities in Christ? Of course, we will not have a heart for someone unless God gives that person to us. Jesus did not pray for all people when he was here on earth, but the Father gave him only a set number. It must be the same for us. People come into the Kingdom of God, one person at a time. And unless the Father draws them, they can't come in.

We have a supernatural foe out to turn our life upside down. He is a master at souring our basic attitudes and creating widespread dysfunction. We need others. The Bible makes this clear.

the power of agreement

"Two are better than one; because they have a good reward for their labour." ~*Ecclesiastes 4: 9*

This whole book of Ecclesiastes is about vanity. The overall point brilliantly made by King Solomon is vital to understand. We all tend to take ourselves so seriously. Our number one task is to love God. The second is our neighbor as ourselves. Yet so many don't seem to love themselves. So how can such a person really love others? Did you know self-hatred and rejection are at the heart of many serious diseases? If we cannot love others in spite of their faults, which were born inside our own families, who can we love? If we do not like someone, and I can understand not naturally being drawn to certain people, then look at them when avoidance is not possible as temporary ministry assignments from God until they are removed from your life.

Satan has done a job on a number of the younger generation (millennials). Many of them seem too alone, self-focused, and are not prone to taking any advice from others, especially their elders. Picture a millennial with a friend and on their phone doing research while seemingly ignoring their close at hand acquaintance! That in a nutshell shows the problem of many today. Do they really understand the importance of loving God and of being a friend? It seems to me that they do not. Satan is the master of the tactic of division. To be with someone and still be alone in your thoughts and actions is very divisive.

The 40% of that generation that is in their parent's basements drowning in anger or debt and living on their smartphones with no real friends in their lives presents a major challenge that must be addressed and overcome at the community level if our nation is to survive. It is beyond most families' ability to correct. This 40% are too important an asset for a nation to just write off as unsalvageable. Maybe some kind of national boot camp is needed.

God is, of course, able supernaturally to fix what needs fixing in their lives. However, that they are 30% less likely than their peers 30 years ago to see religion as important, I see potential as a good thing.

Religion is clearly not the answer. Jesus never preached religion but a kingdom message. The answer is a personal relationship with a royal king. This is the answer. How do we wake them up to the importance of the spiritual world? We cannot! But God can. That means more time in prayer and intercession for those given to you by God.

differing approaches

Many parents seem to hover over their adult children as if they are still children and not responsible. That is a very unhealthy style of leadership. The number one complaint of the young is over supervision. Of course, there are many dangers for young people, as smart in some ways as they seem to be! They can be so unaware. And their lack of appreciation of the importance of supervision is quite challenging for their appointed leaders. But hover over them? Not good! Rather than obsessing over how to help them, we need to see that the real solution is a relationship with Jesus Christ. He is the breaker. Many are shut down in the area of their need for such a salvation. Yet, many are bound up in poor habits and behaviors and do need saving. Reasoning with them usually does not help. Intercessory prayer is the answer. No reasoning or arguments will persuade them.

"The breaker is come up before them: they have broken up, and have passed through the gate, and are gone out by it: and their king shall pass before them, and the LORD on the head of them." ~Micah 2:13

416 times the word "break" is used. A study of this word in scripture is insightful. Here we learn the Breaker is the LORD God. With many millennials, we need his help. At some point, millennials will be positioned and who the nation

must turn to for critical leadership and survival. We see that two are better than one, and a threefold cord is not easily broken. So, there is power in coming together we see from scripture. At least one of the two or three most important relationships in one's life needs to be a person of prayer and faith. If a parent, grandparent, brother, or sister gives up on a family member and no longer prays, then it is not as likely that one outside the family is likely to take up such a difficult burden. Do we really want to see family members on the streets? In most families, I hope no. But! Maybe this is what needs to happen to shock the most stubbornly obstinate into real change.

Speaking of those on the streets: maybe it is time to round them up and put them into some kind of boot camp environment to see who can be cleaned up and who can not. Because of very real difficulties and handicaps, some need our mercy and more structured help. The truly disabled and mentally disturbed cannot help themselves and need our mercy. Those with serious addictions need external discipline and to be motivated by love to change.

the power of a good spouse

Let us talk about the importance of wives and husbands before attacking the subject of tasks more specifically. God tells us:

"And the LORD God said, It is not good that the man should be alone, I will make him an help meet for him."
~Genesis 2: 18

A good wife (or husband) should be a gift to the other. But we see that is not the case in many marriages. I look around today and see a lot of couples that look good from the outside, but who knows what is going on inside their homes and hearts. Divorce is so easy these days. There is a war raging to destroy marriages and families. Look at what the world says about the importance of institutions. We hear about the Fed, the Presidency, Congress, and such, but rarely a word about the family or marriage as vital institutions. Yet it is our most important institution, and it is being torn apart. Much of the government shows little or no real respect for the role of parents in families.

The separation of tasks between married couples use to be clear-cut. Look at our culture today. Who is being trained up to be the "help mate?" When a wife works outside the home, the responsibility for essential tasks at home gets really blurred. Society clearly does not value stay-at-home moms or homeschooling. Life is not as simple as it used to be when I graduated high school in 1958. The balance of tasks that use to exist between husbands and wives seems hardly possible today. Nuclear families! Are there any left? This is not a silly question. A serious national priority should be how to shore up family life. An impossibility without the church. Of course, some are called to the single life, and that is a good thing.

Christ's disciples and our nation

At the first coming of Jesus Christ, the Roman Empire, in many ways, had achieved many wonders. As a nation, they had many different tasks to accomplish to become the great world empire of their day. Their roads and bridges on which their armies marched were amazing. Also, the shipping in which they ruled the seas and traded with faraway nations! They brought in and maintained unity and peace by brute force to counter the savages they faced beyond Roman borders. If that society had not largely rejected Jesus Christ, I wonder if the Huns and the many pagans they had to contend with could have ever overrun them? But they did reject Jesus Christ. And persecuted his disciples who followed after him! There was much Christian martyrdom and 1,000 years of religious darkness that followed. Look at the state of things across Europe today, and European spiritual compromise and hostility have opened the door wide to the spread of Islam while many Europeans have turned their backs on Christianity.

Compare this with what is going on in America. We are the World's mightiest power today, as was Rome in its day. But it is not our armies that win and lose wars, but what a nation allows and does within. Today across the world, anywhere you look, you find traces of America's power: Our American embassies, enterprises, tourists, and our military! Our military reflects what is going on in the nation. Yes, we have spread our influence over a vast area of the earth, as did Rome in its day. But everywhere we look today, we see division. Why? For the same reason, the Roman Empire crumbled; we are now crumbling. We have largely as a people turned our backs on Jesus Christ and are heading into hedonism, humanism, witchcraft, and pleasures just as did the once great Roman Empire. The mind and heart of America are not where they should be. So, if believers are to survive in this culture, we must pick up our Bibles and learn from the successes and mistakes of those believers inside the Roman culture; some were martyred while others survived and prospered two thousand years ago. Yes, the infighting and division across America in places is growing worse. This divisive spirit does not bode well for the nation's future. But we have a hope within us that should motivate us that all is well for us in spite of the chaos we see all around us.

Bible prophecy is quite clear where the world is headed and that it is not our job assignment to save the world. Those who study the Bible will find that about one-fourth of it is prophesied or future history! But most Americans are not readers and so will not discover this vital fact and so will be caught up in what is going on around them. So, they are in for a shock. Who is chapter eighteen of the Book of Revelation speaking of? Many scholars think it is talking about the sudden destruction of a great world empire. The only one that fits that description is America.

the power of two

In Luke chapters 9 and 10, we see where Jesus sent first the twelve and then the 72 out two and two. The Marine Corp's fire teams consist of four men: when this team comes under fire, they are sent in rushes two and two. Or if the enemy fire gets really intense. One will rush forward while three lay down, covering fire for him. For believers, their prayers should be more powerful than angry words directed at them. This is especially true when their prayers combine with the spiritual agreement of one or two other believers. In the dimension of spiritual warfare, one's actions covered by another believer's prayer is very powerful. Why did Jesus set the example of sending out two men when one might have gotten the job done? He knew it was a hostile world. One would need to be in prayer while the other accomplished the necessary task. Here we see the need for a prayer mate.

Who stays back? Who goes out? In our present culture, it is sometimes easier for a talented woman to find work than a talented man. Sad! Is the Bible outdated? Is the man called to be the helpmeet now where circumstances warrant it? Many in the compromised church would say yes. That is not what scripture says. Nor is it God's best for us!

In the home, physical strength is usually not as important as outside of the home; each must be in good physical shape. Stable emotions do depend on good physical health. Both husband and wife benefit from exercise and healthy eating habits. Both men and women have the task of staying in good shape. When either one lets himself go, it hurts the marriage for sure.

Many millennials don't realize the critical balance that must be maintained between the physical, emotional, and spiritual parts of our human nature. Across America, I see an alarming increase in the physical size of people. This is due to several factors: Birth control pills and hormones in milk are apparent contributors, not to mention fast food establishments and GMO foods. Then there is more time sitting in front of television screens and less interest in outside activities that burn off calories such as walking and exercise; this was not the case forty years ago.

spiritual fitness

A great and incredibly famous general who is long since dead and most likely in hell said:

"The moral is to the physical as three to one."
Napoleon Bonaparte

He was a fearless warfighter and is frequently quoted in studies about the nature of war, such as in discussions about strategy and tactics. He had a great mind. I think the proof that much success in life does not lead to heaven. He likely ended up in hell due to his consuming passion for war. He was the conqueror of Europe in his day. Like most great warfighters, he eventually ran up against God Almighty and lost. If you study history, you know the names of many such men: Genghis Kahn, Bismarck, Hitler, Mao, Stalin, etc. They conquered their worlds but lost their souls! This is why, in a discussion on fitness, one's spiritual disposition is of such importance.

Why should we desire and pursue spiritual fitness? Well... does not it make common sense? Apparently not. The majority do not and never will have a personal relationship with Jesus Christ. Look at a list of successful atheists and agnostics who have had significant influence in the world. Many died, never knowing or confessing Jesus Christ as Savior. Men like Marx, whose works are still widely studied even today. Many committed suicide or suffered from illness in their later years. So many never considered they were wrong and likely went into hell due to their stubbornness and pride. They obviously never surrendered their lives to Him. They missed out on the greatest gift of all. No fame or fortune or accomplishment or happiness in this life is worth losing one's salvation. They chased fool's gold.

the great change

The Bible tells us: *"We must be born again." ~**John 3, 3, 6***

They never saw or learned the value of accepting Jesus and his blood sacrifice for us so they could obtain eternal life. They chased fool's gold! That is what most of the world is doing. What folly! Of course, there is more to the life of Christ than spending eternity in heaven with God once we die. Once we are saved, why does God keep us here on this troubled planet? Of course, to help spread the good news that gives others a chance to come to the saving knowledge of Jesus Christ! Why would anyone not listen to such wonderful news? Pure stubbornness prevents many from ever doing so; what a terrible curse. And it is evident in a growing number of the younger people. Thank God there are still so many wonderful young people.

But they need to see far more boldness in seniors who believe the good news. We need to pique their curiosity with our testimonies of God's goodness how he has helped us overcome our demons. With our testimony of his faithfulness. And when we share this good news, signs do-follow. We get to see healings and miracles. Everyone is attracted to the real power of God. They desire to see healings and miracles! When they see you overcoming personal problems and difficulties, they want to learn how it is possible. And you get to tell them of the power of Jesus Christ. Many will listen. And when this happens, he gets the credit.

The most extraordinary task after personal salvation is to help others to overcome. Life is not a cakewalk for anyone.

Of course, you will be resisted by the powers of hell. But you have the victory when you don't get into doubt, fear, and unbelief.

"Submit yourselves, therefore, to God. Resist the devil, and he will flee from you." ~James 4:7

life is less simple these days

I want to motivate readers to investigate the subject of spiritual warfare beyond the limited scope of this book. We need to see that spiritual fitness is critical to our families and us and the nation. The wise allot time to stay fit and healthy no matter the business of their lives. We envy those who set goals and accomplish them. Those who maintain high personal standards are to be commended. How to get there is the question and problem. It takes reflection. What personal priorities need changing to bring more balance into our lives? We know the importance of personal discipline in the quest for excellence. So why do so many continually fall short in certain areas? Where can we do better? Could we be resisted in ways we know not of and need to increase our prayer time?

From personal experience, I can tell you turning to Christ, seeking God and his help is the answer, but seems to be the last thing we think to do. Why is that? The forces of hell know that it means trouble for them when you are continually looking to Christ and his Holy Spirit.

So, we are resisted in powerful, devious ways. Satan is clever. He knows how to camouflage his actions and influence. You will blame yourself or others when he is behind something. Only if you are ready and studying scripture closely and seeking God's presence do you begin to understand why you do the things you do. When you genuinely start putting God first all the time, after testing to see if you are really serious about walking in the light of Christ, God steps towards you in ways that leave no doubt he loves you. And Satan flees to wait for another opening to make mischief.

"And so, after he had patiently endured, he obtained the promise."~ **Hebrews 6:15**

Our task as overcomers is to increase our effectiveness in using the warfighting skills that are available to us in the Lord's mighty overcoming army. There are so many different tasks that we should never grow bored in serving the LORD. Finding those who will listen to our testimonies of Christ's faithfulness should occupy us until he returns as promised.

"And they went forth, and preached everywhere, the Lord working with them, and confirming the word with signs following, Amen." ~**Mark 16:20**

37906

7

ESPRIT de CORPS

It is human nature: people want to be a part of something big and exciting. When I was young, like many, I wanted to make a difference. As a young boy watching the birds, I can remember acting out a desire to fly. I would pretend I was superman. Can you remember such a time? When we are young and innocent, dreaming is a beautiful gift. Imaginations are such a wonderful creation. What did you want to come true that never did? Life can trample on otherwise achievable dreams. By middle school, you can see who has been messed with in some way and who has not. Their posture, behavior, and dress scream out a message. Of course, we all can blame others when we fall short. It is an easy thing to do. But our own inability to discipline ourselves through study, focus, overcoming distractions, and saying no to the temptations of friends is a huge part of achieving childhood dreams.

Of course, many do have a rough hand early on: a family member or neighborhood bullies, etc.: When kids leave their home, there are unhealthy external influences galore: gangs, drugs, and such. Non-family teachers and mentors are essential and can fill a gap. But there are not enough such people. We all run into those that, for whatever reason, hold us back. They can change the direction we secretly want to go in if we let them. Those close to us can discourage us. It is tough to live with such persons inside our own homes.

I wonder! Is that why superhero movies are so popular? Are they just entertaining and fun? Or could they be touching something deep inside us? We fantasize about what superhumans can do and accomplish. Things impossible and beyond our reach in real life! But to really make a difference in this world is not easy these days. Until stifled, it seems to be a drive for most of us. Why? Because we are made in the image of God. It is not hard to really dream big but achieving on a grand scale is something else. Life presents us with many challenges to overcome. We either overcome them and move toward our goals, or problems overcome us.

challenges

This chapter title is the motto of Marines. It recognizes a basic truth. There is a force or spirit that can be activated. One key to overcoming power; individually and collectively! Few at the beginning of any great work have a faithful spirit or great confidence within them, to begin with. But we are all attracted to those who do have such a spirit within. Organizations that exude this overcoming power are great places to work. Such power becomes a living force that is felt and seen by others. Such an atmosphere is a real force, be it positive or negative in its long-term effect. It can take on a life of its own. Like faith, it grows or shrinks. The Marine Corps cultivates this spirit. It covets it. And for the nation, it is a good thing.

For its size, the Marine Corps is arguably the greatest warfighting force in history. It would not remain such a great fighting organization for long if a lesser nation's ideals than America were standing behind it. If America sold the Marine Corps to any other nation, it would not garner the same respect for very long. American exceptionalism still stands behind it. Marines that believe we are an exceptional nation make exceptional fighters. They don't think like mercenaries, and that is a good thing.

America has been an extraordinary world power. A superpower! Arguably several nations ganging up against us might be able to bring us down. To overpower us! But I think this nation can only be taken down from within. We are seeing citizens in powerful positions of influence, trying to do that very thing. Why because they believe in globalism. They no longer believe in the sovereignty of nations or American exceptionalism. They are for new world order. They want to look to one reigning power like the U.N. headed up by one man. And the Bible says this will happen. A growing number of people don't want God ruling over them. And for a season, they will get their wish.

There are spiritual prophecies, dreams, and visions posted on the internet that tell us America will not be around during the coming Great Tribulation discussed in the last book of the Bible. It is hard for many to imagine this could ever be true. For years I have been led to pray that America will be found to be a sheep nation, not one of the goat nations at the end of days. We see from the Old Testament that God created 70 nations. He wants to save nations, not just individuals. Why? Because he is a loving God. He knows that righteous nations impact their citizens and families for good. Evil rulers harm them. One evil man will rule the coming one-world government. He will do great harm. God does not want that. So, he is for nations, not a one-world government. But the world's people will clamor for a human savior. This, of course, will change in the millennial reign when God returns to earth to rule and reign.

America does not have the largest standing army. China does. But it would be hard-pressed right now to reach our shores without the help of neighboring nations. We do not have as significant a number of naval ships as at the end of WWII. We don't have as many planes either. But the ones we do have pack greater firepower. We have started to develop a space force that we don't hear much about. We certainly do not have the greatest population in terms of numbers. We are not the only nuclear power in the world. Many nations outside our borders have real power too. But it is the doubters and schemer inside our borders we need to be concerned about.

Why are Americans who don't know God so confident in a united nation's government of men? Are such people deceived? Arguably the Book of **Revelation, chapter 18** is a prophecy about America. If that prophecy is about us, our coming destruction will occur in one hour. This is God's Word of the future, and right now, it fits only our nation. Many believe our nation is still under the protection of God. The leaders of ancient Israel believed this until right around the time the Rome army destroyed Jerusalem and scatter the Jews to the ends of the earth. This occurred around 68-70 A.D. They could not see that God had departed before that terrible point in time. Has God written Ichabod on our Constitution and departed, but we have not seen the final effect of that departure yet? When Israel, the apple of God's eye, turned their backs on God, he humbled them and destroyed their nation. But he promised to regather that nation, bringing it back into existence in 1948. The Jews recaptured Jerusalem in 1967. This was prophesized by Ezekiel thousands of years before it happened. President Trump declared in 2018 that Jerusalem was their nation's capital. We were the first to move our embassy there.

Why is this history important to us? It is likely a shadow of things to come. Right now, we are that city on a hill providing gospel light to the world. But our light is growing dim. Unlike most other nations, we still have the

Holy Spirit in our midst. I believe that Spirit is at the heart of true esprit de corps in our important institutions. The Holy Ghost right now is the secret weapon of believers and of the institutions they support! Until it departs at the rapture of the believers (**II Thessalonians 2:7**)! That is why we remain the number one destination in the world for immigrants. Where else would they go for the opportunity and freedom we still offer? Their nations too often lack this important esprit de corps that can still be found in many of our giving organizations.

an explanation

Esprit de Corps is a feeling of pride, fellowship, and exceptional loyalty based on a history of real accomplishment in the face of trying conditions. In spite of those who hate America and are trying to bring us down, there are still more of us who love this nation and will fight for it than those within who want a different world order. They support the corrupt United Nations and want to make it the one ruling power on earth. They are very good at screaming, hating, and making a lot of noise to accomplish their goals. Unfortunately, many buy into their logic and plan. Their negative enthusiasm is not what I write about here, though. Zeal is seldom the core of a true esprit de corps. A wrong spirit is behind their motives. Theirs is a spirit of destruction and hatred. Of course, they will tell you otherwise.

What is "esprit de corps" all about? In the 2nd Marine Division based in Camp Lejeune, North Carolina, the Commanding General, twenty years ago anyway, had various indicators of the division's warfighting readiness based on different tests and evaluations. One of these indicators was the level of "esprit de corps" or unity in the fighting forces under his command. He looked at different factors to determine this fighting spirit, such as morale, low absenteeism, low unit punishment rates, and high physical fitness scores to tally up his overall level of unit readiness. He considered many different factors: about 72 to see where a unit was at concerning overall readiness to deploy. I never served in this particular Marine Division, but one of my sons did. When I visited the headquarters building while visiting him many years ago, I saw the readiness status board. I am just writing about it from memory. Confidence is a critical thing for individuals and units in coping with the stresses and strains of life. Before a unit is deployed, it spends its days' training, testing, inspecting, and bringing it up to and maintained at the commander's level of expectation who commands it.

the spirit

Another way of saying esprit de corps is "spirit of unity." When you enter a new organization, you often feel a different spirit from the last place you were. Another way of talking about "the spirit" is if your high school got a new principal. When that person takes over, the atmosphere can change noticeably and quickly for better or worse. Spirits are real. When a new leader takes over, he or she can bring in a different ruling spirit. The spirit of the leader brings about change for good or bad.

When we look at a man or woman, we see a physical body with a personality. That person is more than a body. Each of us has a soul and a spirit. When a person dies, the soul and spirit depart and go somewhere else. The Bible tells us to heaven or hell. You see this in the testimonies of people with near-death experiences posted on the internet. When the real person departs, the body is now considered dead. It is no longer that person. What remains is like a suit. The person steps out, and there is an emptiness that can be felt or sensed concerning the suit. Do you know what I am trying to say?

who stands with you

Suppose you are a private in the army. In that case, a fire team leader stands behind you along with a chain of command above that supports the team, a squad leader, a platoon commander, a company commander, a battalion commander, a regimental commander, a division commander, a corps commander, and the nation—hopefully, all the leaders of that nation, and hopefully, God, above all. You get the picture. If the private's authority and power are not sufficient to do the job he was ordered to do, he can appropriate more power from the authority just above him. Who stands behind you in your domain? If you are in an army, it is quite clear. It is even clear in most cases for any righteous citizen. Who stands behind you in a fight is very important to the outcome.

"God is a Spirit and they that worship him must worship him in spirit and in truth."~John 4:24

We are speaking of "esprit" or spirit! Whether a military member, a new citizen of the United States, or an elected official like a mayor or governor, we are all taking the same oath swearing loyalty to our nation's U.S. Constitution. When we are sworn in, we take an oath of allegiance. For illegal immigrants, they cannot just cross our national border and stand in line for handouts. And mayors should not treat riots like peaceful protests. Traitors in leadership are easy to see.

Also, in the army of God, we must pledge our allegiance if we want to be treated like family. Jesus told Nicodemus, a righteous Jew and member of the Sanhedrian, that *"we must be born again."* Why would Jesus tell us this? It must be important to be *"born again."*

It is not enough to say we are Christians because our parents were. If you were born into a Christian family and raised up as a Christian, still at some point as an adult, you must affirm your faith publicly. Most religious Christians say they love Jesus. And many seem to be decent, kind people. So why must they be born again?

I see churchgoers come into the church on Sunday mornings. They sit in the pews, sing the songs, listen to the sermon, and when dismissed, leave until next week. For many, attendance is a duty or habit like going to work: something that reasonable people just do. But has their heart been changed by a lifelong practice that started when they were carried into church as infants? Are they excited as a Christian? Do they look to share Christ beyond the church door? Is this the number one subject they enjoy talking about? Is there a sense of brotherhood when they, by chance, meet another believer? For most church members, I would say no unless they have been born again or have something personal in common! When you are really born again, you remember when and where it happened. I do.

How are we born again? In the upper room after the departure of Jesus back to heaven, 120 troubled disciples of Jesus gathered to wait for the promise of the Father. This was what they were instructed to do. After ten days of seeking, waiting, and prayer, tongues of fire fell on them. They were all filled with the Holy Spirit. They spoke in tongues. Then they went out into the streets and could not keep quiet about what had happened. They were accused of being drunk by those not in the upper room because of their uninhibited excitement. They were not the same. This is what being born again is all about: radical change: a new beginning!

why needed

I have a theory about why we must be born again. Look at the state of the world. Evil is everywhere. Things are so bad that even those who do not believe in God are desperate to see real change. There is a doomsday clock ticking down run by non-religious secularists. The elites talk about the need for population reduction to save the planet. They earnestly promote the need for birth control and abortion. They talk about global warming as if it is a life-or-death matter.

Watching Christians see the signs that Jesus warned about in Matthew 24, Mark 13, and Luke 21 approaching.

Here Jesus talked directly about the signs of his return. Wars and rumors of wars, etc. He said it would be like in the days before the flood, the days of Noah. What was it like then? Only evil continually! The sons of God had come down and cohabitated with the daughters of men creating the Nephilium or offspring (hybrids). Mighty men but not entirely human! Scripture tells us they all were not wiped out by the flood but again reproduced. Today we read about scientists tampering with human DNA in the news. Crosses between humans and animals to create more perfect humans, super soldiers. It says in scripture:

"And the LORD said unto Noah, Come thou and all thy house into the ark; for thee have I seen righteous before me in this generation."~ **Genesis 7:1**

Looking at the Hebrew meaning here for the word righteous, we see it was not talking here about moral purity, but about the fact, Noah's DNA was not tainted by what the fallen angels had done with the daughters of men. Sexual impurity! A change in the DNA. The rest of humanity's downline was no longer fully human.

Could it be again we all at birth have corrupted DNA from the fallen angels and need to be born again to reverse the effect of what the Nephelium have done since the flood and are doing today through evil men? I think this is possible. Look at how hard it is to change our natures by just trying to be good like Jesus, whose blood was not corrupted. We all need a superhuman assist from God, it seems. We know that Jesus had to come into this world as a human and live a sinless life to give us hope and a chance to be saved. Why was this necessary? Because of what Satan had done and is still doing in secret.

We see the work of the organized church how it is falling short of bringing about real change. I am certainly not against churches. But while the Christian religion does many good works, the key to real change in human nature is the *"born again"* experience. That is why I think Jesus said, *"you must be born again."*

noticeable change

Real change occurs when one is genuinely through with the way he is, is desperate for change, and surrenders his life to God. Something similar happens in the transformation a military boot camp brings about in most civilians. Most recruits are changed by the process, step into a new life, and walk in a new direction during their enlistment.

Everyone can see the change. Witnesses of the change will say something like: "What has happened to you?" There is a new boldness, changes in past habits such as no more need for tobacco or no longer having a foul mouth. Something very noticeable happens that shows people there has been a real change. For me, my hunger and thirst for reading daily from God's Word, and a new boldness for Christ, was evidence enough for me that I had been truly changed and saved.

the other side

A demonic army is also being built. They also believe in "esprit de corps." While the shrinking majority of humanity is in the balance and has not yet fully committed to either side, all must choose sides in this battle in the end. The elite and their secret societies make their plans in secret and try to carry them out in a not-so-secret way. When they gain sufficient control, they come out in the open like with this Covid-19 orchestrated pandemic exercise which has been planned for decades. At some point, they will gain the power to prevail and dominant for a short time. Behind the scenes, there is a real battle going on right now for control. I have not seen the likes since people took sides over the Vietnam War. This battle began in the heavens long ago but is spilling on to the earth in a frightening way. People in the know, know what is going on. Most of us do not have a clue unless we study prophesy to see how daily national and international news stories might confirm biblical prophecy.

All of us are born in sin. Our natures have been corrupted by the sin of parents and grandparents all the way back to Adam and Eve's original sin. Satan and his demonic realm have the advantage. We not only have to battle his evil forces but our own sin natures too. That is why God had to come to earth to save us. We are not capable of saving ourselves. We are now seeing a real increase in witchcraft, witches, and warlocks. We see this interest in the attendance of movies about this dark side. Books like the Harry Potter series and television shows about witches, hexes, spells, and such are growing by leaps and bounds.

There is a certain level of power over others by people who choose the dark side. Satan is the god of this world. He does give a form of energy to those who submit to him. But God's power is far greater when used. We do see a satanic enthusiasm evident in those who love darkness. They are excited when a new movie promotes their interests. The lines outside the theaters to attend their movies are longer than the lines to see our movies, like LUTHER, RISEN, GOD's NOT DEAD, and WAR ROOM, to name a few.

outward appearance

Some Christians wear a cross around their necks or put a sign of a fish on their cars or decorate their yards with a manger during Christmas. While a bold thing to do to show allegiance, it is a religious act for many. What happens inside a person, the transformation, once born again, is what really matters? What we do with our outward appearance is secondary. As we mature in Christ, we should become more modest and more humble. Hard to do on our own! Disciplined people can make subtle changes in their outward appearance over time and improve their personalities in better ways for sure. But most need to see a real character change before they are impressed enough to say what happened to you.

familiar spirits

The work of Satan has affected each of our bloodlines. That is why we all must come under the bloodline of Jesus Christ to be saved. Only then will there be sufficient grace to overpower what the enemy attempts to do in each of us through the lust of the flesh, the lust of the eyes and the pride of life.

Familiar spirits work our bloodlines. Open doors because of sin invite them into our lives through personal sin. Or because of the sin of parents or grandparents, they already have entered our lives. These spirits are powerful. They work in secret. We think their influence is just part of who we are. A propensity to drink, or swear, or be jealous, or to anger, or a taste for hard liquor, etc.! Name the sin, and spirits are promoting these appetites. These are real spirits without bodies. They are not easily detected or discovered. Most people never become aware of them, so never suspect their influence over them. They just think it is just the way I am. A spiritual deliverance or years of professional clinical help to overcome a hated habit or weakness is required to change. And still, most people who have such familiar spirits controlling them never change and begin to think suicide is their only out: another familiar spirit. Most have no idea that a spiritual deliverance is a solution.

Psych wards are full of such people. Psychologists make their living trying to help people who hate themselves. Deep down, many troubled people know that is not who they are when they act out of character. Still, so many stubbornly never turn to Christ, or if they do, do not have a pastor who knows how to help them. Why are some children seemingly bad out of the womb? Or normal for years until they suddenly change? Could it be the effects of generational sin and familiar spirits? The answer is yes.

"Keeping mercy for thousands, forgiving iniquity and transgression and sin and that will by no means clear the guilty; visiting the iniquity of the fathers upon the children, and upon their children's children, unto the third and to the fourth generation." ~Exodus 34:7

I Peter, chapter four is all about living in the Spirit. Of course, no one who is not born again can do this. Jesus Christ, who was born perfect, was subjected to his parents and under their authority as we all are when young. At the age of thirty, he was baptized by John at the Jordan River, and the Holy Ghost came upon him. Of course, Jesus was fully God and did not have to be born again. He already had a divine nature. But set the example for us. This example alone is proof enough; we all need to be born again. The fact that we were born into a good Christian family and raised up in the church is not enough.

Jesus demonstrated esprit de corps with his Father in heaven. He always did what pleased his father. He only did what his father showed him to do. Though he was flesh and blood like us, he lived in the Spirit. We are told to be like him. He walked in the Spirit of Liberty. We can too.

Do you know the Holy Spirit? More importantly, does He inhabit you?

There is an esprit de corps among those who are born again. We, increasingly in this evil world, recognize and are drawn to each other. Our spirits are lifted when we are around other true believers. We love each other and feel closer with those who love Christ than our own blood relations who are not born again. Of course, we want to see all our blood family come to Christ and should pray to that effect. Living this exciting life in the Spirit is truly an adventure! We pray they will see the light and become part of God's own family. It is the best gift possible one could wish for another. But it is a choice each of us must make on our own. High morale should be easy to come by and keep when troubles come to a believer. Knowing we are on the winning side is a great comfort and advantage in this life.

"And such as do wickedly against the covenant shall he corrupt by flatteries: but the people that do know their God shall be strong and do exploits." ~**Daniel 11:32**

Our enemies also have their own kind, as this verse above indicates. We who are alert and watching see the deep state corruption that is going on. However, the vast majority are still asleep and caught in the middle of this increasingly deadly struggle going on. They cannot see the real situation, or if they do, don't know what to do about it. The double-minded are troubled in all their ways. Everyone must choose sides in this struggle for souls. Whose side are you on? Where does your enthusiasm really lie? With the world or with Jesus Christ? What truly excites you...?

8

ENTANGLEMENTS

"Lolita C. Baldor of the Associated Press reported in an article July 13, 2011, that CIA Director Gen. Davis Petraeus who wrote a book titled ALL IN: The Education of General David Petraeus, coauthored by biographer Paula Broadwell, resigned on November 9, 2012 citing an extramarital affair with Broadwell. In another article, I saw the Associated Press reported Brig. Gen. Jeffrey Sinclair was fired from his command in Afghanistan in May and was facing a court-martial on charges of sodomy, adultery, and pornography. These two reports are just two in a long line of commanders whose careers were ended because of possible sexual misconduct. Sex has proved to be the downfall of presidents, members of Congress, and other notables. It is also among the chief reasons senior military officers are fired. According to statistics compiled by The Associated Press, at least 30 percent of military commanders fired over the past eight years lost their jobs because of sexually related

offenses, including harassment, adultery, and improper relationships. The figures bear out growing concerns by Defense Department and military leaders over declining ethical values among U. S. forces, and they highlight the pervasiveness of a problem that came into sharp relief because of the resignation of one of the Army's most esteemed generals, David Petraeus, and the investigation of a second general, John Allen, the top U.S. commander in Afghanistan. The statistics from all four military services show that adulterous affairs are more than a four-star foible. From sexual assault and harassment to pornography, drugs and drinking, ethical lapses are an escalating problem for the military's leaders. Eighteen generals and admirals, from one star to four stars, were fired in recent years, and 10 of them lost their jobs because of sex-related offenses; two others were done in by alcohol-related problems."

unholy entanglements

Entanglements can happen to true believers. But once the new birth has translated them from darkness to light, they must decide to go back into darkness for such entanglements to exist. God gives us discernment and spiritual tools to resist the wiles of the enemy. This article above is one of many about the problem of unholy entanglements. I expect this general who had a great career was exposed to right and wrong growing up and had a good reputation as far as I can tell among those who served with him. So, what happened?

We find this word *"entangle"* in the Bible only five times. Though not used often in the Bible, look at its synonyms. Interactions between people can quickly get messy and complicated. A believer discerning the dangers must always be on guard. Satan does not play fair. This subject is a critical discussion to have when looking at the issue of spiritual warfare. The Cambridge Dictionary definition is cryptic: *"a situation or relationship involved in that is difficult to escape from."* Some synonyms are involvement, intrigue, complication, mix-up, undertaking, affair, relationship, fling, and flirtation! These words help paint a picture of the "pickle" people get themselves into when they forsake the Bible's moral compass for one of their own makings. Daily we must be aware of Satan's devices and put on the armor of God. **(Ephesians 6:11-18)**

Entanglements do more than complicate people's lives and relationships. They end up ruining them. There is something worse that happens as they move forward: self-imposed blindness. How does Satan get otherwise bright people into such a mess? One way is through the use of distraction. He first distracts us by diverting our focus to get us to trip and fall into the pit of deception.

We purpose to live a godly life. He distracts us; we get confused or sidetracked and find ourselves doing or getting involved in something which we would never purpose to do on our own. How is this possible? He puts a thought in our minds. If not summarily dismissed, it can tumble right out of our mouth at an inappropriate moment, starting a sequence of events with no real thought of the consequence. And then we begin to own actions we might have sworn we would never do. Maybe it was not our thought to start. But over time, if we are not careful, it becomes ours. It points us down a different path than the one we intended to walk. Was the whole thing a demonic entrapment? Has this happened to you or someone you care about? Satan tries to work such tactics against all of us, especially believers.

the seductive nature of entanglements

In Chu Lai, Vietnam, in 1965, my battalion lost a popular officer, a major, to the sea. He was due to rotate home the next day, the end of his three-year overseas tour. He was walking on the rocks at the edge of the South Vietnam seashore enjoying its beauty, probably looking for souvenirs to take home to his kids. A rogue wave came in unexpectedly, knocking him off his feet. The backwash took him seaward. I never hear whether his body was found. He was married with four children.

I pondered why this could happen. I remembered his behavior when a group of us were in Taiwan on liberty from Okinawa before we were deployed into Vietnam. He had a liaison with a prostitute from Thailand that he knew during a prior tour. Did he have a character defect? God didn't want him taking back home to a praying wife. Terrible venereal diseases were going around that we had all been warned about that could not be cured. We all were warned about the dangers of lying with prostitutes.

Because of the talk the day before our liberty run to Taipei, I covenanted with a believing friend that we would hang out together so neither of us would be pulled into what some of the other officers were looking forward to engaging in. Such experiences change a man forever. I wanted no part of it. The book of Proverbs speaks early about wisdom. There are apparent warnings against lying with strange women. Haven't most men and women been exposed to those who discard such warnings? If not careful, such predilections can suck us into something ugly…. Before we know it, we are entangled in a bad situation that only gets worse.

Remember David and Bathsheba. How he got entangled with a married woman. After all the great things God had done in his life! It could have taken him out permanently. Because of a prophet's intervention and his resulting deep repentance, his relationship with God was restored. But there were severe lifelong consequences. He lived the rest of his life dealing with problems in the family because of his poor judgment in a moment of weakness. His sin set in motion happenings in his family line and Kingdom that were not good and continue to plague Israel today. Actions like adultery and murder always affect others. This sad story is told in **II Samuel chapter four**.

Other people's entanglements can also affect us adversely. Who has not heard the word co-dependency? Many people suffered because of David's sin and inappropriateness. He was in a position of power, the king of a nation. This entanglement had a great impact across the land. Most of us have nowhere near his position or influence in society. But each of us is part of a family and should take no such risks because of the resulting harm to those we profess to love who are dependent on us.

an enemy tactic

We see in **Matthew 22:15** where entanglement is an actual tactic of the enemy:

"Then went the Pharisees and took counsel how they might entangle him in his talk."

They were trying to entrap Jesus so they could kill him. The next few verses tell the story and how Jesus outwitted them.

We see in **Galatians 5:1** how we can avoid being entrapped by this actual spirit of entanglement.

"Stand fast therefore in the liberty wherewith Christ hath made us free, and be not entangled again with the yoke of bondage."

Paul goes on in this chapter to talk about being under the law of sin and death or being under grace. Our choice! Look at *II Timothy 2:4*

"No man that warreth entangleth himself with the affairs of this life; that he may please him who hath chosen him to be a soldier."

Who do you really want to please? The last verse in the New Testament that uses this word really captures for me the importance of understanding the battle we are all in to avoid entanglements:

"For if after they have escaped the pollutions of the world through the knowledge of the Lord and Savior Jesus Christ, they are again <u>entangled</u> therein, and overcome, the latter end is worse with them than the beginning." ~ **II Peter 2:20**

in battle

We are in a battle. Whether we are in the armed forces or a civilian among civilians, we must think like soldiers and look to our commander, Jesus Christ, in everything we do. Don't get entangled with the affairs of this life. Live above the fray. The only way this is possible is to know the scriptures and to cling tightly to Jesus Christ and his Spirit. Otherwise, we will be overcome. Satan wants us to live in the visible world all the time. God exhorts us to live in the invisible world. Only in his kingdom of light are we safe. Avoid slipping back into the kingdom of darkness at all cost.

translated

The Bible uses the word *"translated"* three times. This word gives us a critical understanding of one of the great benefits of being a believer in Christ. The first time we see it used is in **II Samuel,** where we see a power struggle between those who believed in Saul and those who believe in David. A battle for control! This was a life and death struggle for power where those who took sides could die opposing the other side or kingdom. Whose side in those days would you have been on not knowing the outcome? Most of us tend to go along with the status quo. David's side only after a long struggle prevailed. Many automatically side with the majority. This was a kingdom against kingdom struggle. We are in such a struggle today. It is the two uses in the New Testament of this word I want to highlight.

"Who hath delivered us from the power of darkness, and hath <u>translated</u> us into the kingdom of his dear Son...If ye continue in the faith grounded and settled, and be not moved away from the hope of the gospel, which ye have heard, and which was preached to every creature which is under heaven; where of I Paul am made a minister;" ~**Colossians 1;13-23**

"By faith, Enoch was <u>translated</u> that he should not see death; and was not found because God had <u>translated</u> him: for before his <u>translation,</u> he had this testimony, that he pleased God."~ **Hebrews 11:5**

This should be a frequently asked question: do I please God right now? What do I want you to see in these verses about translation? Look at **Colossians 1:13** *"...delivered us from... <u>translated</u> us into..."*

We see in **Hebrews 11:5** above that Enoch because he pleased God, was delivered out of a dangerous world bodily. He just disappeared. He did not experience death! He was translated to heaven! Because of his faith! This is how important our faith is.

One scripture talks about a spiritual translation: the other a physical translation. Could it be if we demonstrate a similar faith in these dangerous times that we could be protected in similar ways because of our having surrendered our life to the LORD? In **Colossians 1:13,** we see two kingdoms are spoken of: the kingdom of darkness and the kingdom of his dear Son. Both exist on earth at the same time where we stand. Satan has power in his kingdom, but not inside God's kingdom.

I have always been puzzled about a verse I have read and studied where Christ in danger from the crowd and its leaders seemed to be supernaturally protected. The thought that I can be protected in the same way Jesus was because of my faith in him is exciting. We know Jesus was special at his first coming. Different from us, but the same in all ways. He put aside his divine powers and became an example for us. The only divine power he used during his ministry was the same power we have when we are baptized in the Holy Ghost and operating in his will. This baptism of Jesus is described once in **Matthew 3:13** and once in **Mark 1:9**. This is an actual divine power that comes down on us who seek it, as He did Jesus. But we must submit and believe in the promised gift from the Father in heaven above. What are some verses I have pondered on? They are verses like this one.

"But when they sought to lay hands on him, they feared the multitude because they took him for a prophet."
~Mathew 21:46

The gospel writers often talked about the anger of the enemies of Jesus. They plotted to kill him and frequently attempted to lay hands on him because of his radical teachings. But when they went to grab him, he would be able to walk through the crowds and go his way. It seems to me that the spirit in his accusers could not touch the Spirit in him. **(I John 4:4)** He never was under their power. At the time determined by the Father, he willingly laid his life down for us. This was the main reason he came to earth so that His blood sacrifice could redeem us!

the coming visitation

There is a man from Israel, a military veteran and reservist with the rank of major in the IDF, who I really admire. He is an outspoken believer in the Lord Jesus Christ. His name is Emir Tsarfadi. He has a ministry called BEHOLD ISRAEL. He travels the world preaching on the Pretribulation rapture, His imminent coming, the need to wake up spiritually, and gives frequent situation updates on the Middle East and Israel.

We know at the first coming of Jesus to this earth that most missed the time of their visitation from God. God uses the word *"visitation"* fifteen times. It is always about judgment. Those who are not awake and watching miss what God is doing and suffer severe consequences. Moses first used this word in **Numbers 16: 28.** It was about a visitation to come on evil men opposing him. Read the passage and be enlightened.

Emir Tsarfadi said something in a news brief conducted in Brazil on October 11, 2019: *"One thing the enemy wants for us is to be asleep."* He pointed out in the city where he was ministering; the 11 million people there have no understanding of the nearness of the rapture or the start of the Great Tribulation. They are asleep. This is the city that has a large statue of Jesus with outstretched arms. It is also the city that has the world's most famous pagan carnival. **Rio de Janeiro!** Many visitors go there looking to get entangled.

scriptural warnings

"And what will ye do in the day of visitation and in the desolation, which shall come from far? To whom will ye flee for help? And where will ye leave your glory?" ~ **Isaiah 10:3**

"Were they ashamed when they had committed abomination? Nay, they were not at all ashamed, neither could they blush: therefore, shall they fall among them that fall in the time of their visitation they shall be cast down, saith the LORD." ~**Jeremiah 8:12**

Jeremiah uses this word eight different times. He tries to warn his people of coming judgment. His warnings fell on deaf ears. The Prophet Hosea uses this word once.

"The days of visitation are come, the days of recompense are come; Israel shall know it: the prophet is a fool, the spiritual man is mad, for the multitude of thine iniquity, and the great hatred." ~**Hosea 9:7**

The Prophet Micah also tried to warn his people:

*"The best of them is as a brier: the most upright is sharper than a thorn hedge: the day of thy watchmen and thy <u>visitation</u> cometh; now shall be their perplexity. Trust ye not in a friend, put ye not confidence in a guide: keep the doors of thy mouth from her that lieth in thy bosom. For the son dishonoureth the father, the daughter riseth up against her mother, the daughter in law against her mother-in-law; a man's enemies are the men of his own house. Therefore, I will look unto the LORD; I will wait for the God of my salvation: my God will hear me."~ **Micah 7:4-7***

Jesus warned the people at his first coming and also those to follow. This age of grace will suddenly end with a visitation (the rapture). Then the prophesized judgment will fall across the whole earth:

*"For the days shall come upon thee, that thine enemies shall cast a trench about thee, and compass thee round, and keep thee in on every side, And shall lay thee even with the ground, and thy children within thee; and they shall not leave in thee one stone upon another; because thou knewest not the time of thy <u>visitation</u>." ~**Luke 19: 43-44***

In Matthew chapter sixteen, we have seen him warning his disciples about not being deceived. God is visiting his people even now, and most are rejecting him.

"The Pharisees also with the Sadducees came, and tempting desired him that he would show them a sign from heaven. He answered and said unto them When it is evening ye say, It will be fair weather; for the sky is red. And in the morning, It will be foul weather today: for the sky is red and lowering. O ye hypocrites, ye can discern the face of the sky, but can ye not discern the signs of the times? A wicked and adulterous generation seeketh after a sign; and there shall no

sign be given unto it, but the sign of the prophet Jonas. And he left them and departed." ~Matthew 16: 1-4

watchmen and prophets

There are a lot more people who tell us good times are coming than bad. Both can be speaking the truth where coming judgment is concerned. There is both good judgment and bad at the same time.

"A thousand shall fall at thy side, and ten thousand at thy right hand; but it shall not come nigh thee."~ Psalms 91:7

This psalm is a favorite among believers inside the military. What awesome protection for the obedient. What a fearful judgment for those out from under God's protection. Many pastors major on the doctrine of prosperity and other pleasant, reassuring messages that can be constructed from the scriptures. But where is the balance? If they never preach on sin, hell, the rapture, tribulation, and second coming of the LORD, are they really deceiving their flock?

The church needs watchmen who are posted at vantage points where they can see the enemy approaching. This is for natural warfare and spiritual too. How many watchmen ever get a chance to give a message in a church pulpit on a Sunday morning? Many in the millennial generation are not prone to listen to those who are older and maybe wiser. Unfortunately, many of their elders have become distracted and entangled with the world. Their faults might be quite visible to those who are younger. With those they have grown up with, they can show no respect. Sad! An entire generation is in danger of being lost through stubborn unbelief. Many know nothing of the prophesized judgment that is coming. They will quickly fall under the spell of the man of sin, the antichrist.

we, too, are tempted

Will most American Christians be as blind at the Second Coming as was Israel 2,000 years ago, when they failed to recognize their messiah? Will most of the church miss the time of America's visitation (the Rapture of the Church)? There is a terrible absence of discernment blinding many in our society. Those who become entangled with life affairs become so absorbed in their own situations that they miss what is going on, the bigger picture! So many today are missing the signs we are told to watch for. Sudden change is coming. For most, it will not be good.

"But of the times and the seasons, brethren, ye have no need that I write unto you. For yourselves know perfectly that the day of the Lord so cometh as a thief in the night. For when they shall say, Peace and safety; then sudden destruction cometh upon them, as travail upon a woman with child; and they shall not escape. But ye, brethren, are not in darkness, that that day should overtake you as a thief. Ye are all the children of light, and the children of the day: we are not of the night, nor of darkness. Therefore, let us not sleep, as do others; but let us watch and be sober."
~I Thessalonians 5: 2-5

In this likely terminal generation, we are living in, we cannot afford to be pulled into such entanglements as took out this popular army general.

We must be on guard, prayerful, and looking up for our redemption draws near, and we do not want to be left behind. Great vigilance is called for in this age of deception.

"And the Lord shall deliver me from every evil work and will preserve me unto his heavenly kingdom: to whom be glory for ever and ever, Amen."
~II Timothy 4:18

9

COMMUNICATING FAITH

Hunger and thirst for reading the Bible came over me when the Holy Ghost filled me four decades into my life. That appetite was not there before the experience that transformed my life. That wonderful night God made himself real to me. It was highly personal. I was well past the age of reason. My understanding of God was religious before this encounter with Jesus Christ left me with a testimony that I could excitedly share.

Growing up in the church, I wanted to please God. But my involvement with spiritual things was more academic, ceremonial, and sacramental. None of this gave me a testimony that would impact anyone. I never led anyone to Christ before this vivid encounter. I was overseas on a military assignment for a year at the time. Until then, I lacked any real boldness to overcome my shyness to testify of my faith in God. I did have a quiet conviction that what I felt about my beliefs were true, but it didn't go anywhere outside, occasionally volunteering at church. I was capable of zeal when prodded. But that kind of boldness really comes from one's head, not from one's heart. There are many prayer promises and scriptures I could share that are important to me now. But for the sake of brevity will keep this chapter brief.

prayer promises

"And all things, whatsoever ye shall ask in prayer, believing, ye shall receive." ~Matthew 21:22

We must have faith that we will receive from God, when we ask. If we pick and choose from the Bible what we do and do not believe, can we really expect God to think we are serious about pleasing him? If I were that way, I would be doubleminded. My prayers would just be a religious ritual.

*"We have to believe that God exists and that he is a rewarder of those who diligently seek him." ~***Hebrews 11:6**

Only then can we expect God to answer us when we pray. Frankly, as a religious Christian though very sincere, I did not consistently have that kind of faith. Yes, there were times when I did press in with mixed results. Acts 4:31 shows that God's power follows real prayers.

"And when they had prayed, the place was shaken where they were assembled together; and they were all filled with the Holy Ghost, and they spake the word of God with boldness."

When I do not see real enthusiasm about the things of God in a churchgoer, I wonder if they are even saved. We can be raised up as Christian and really believe we are in good graces with God because we go to church and hang around with other good people. The Bible does not support this. It is just head knowledge if there has been no true heart-wrenching surrender. Only then will such a person be able to stand firm when the storm comes. I have been in the company of strong-willed unbelievers. Some of them are very nice. For the sake of peace, they might go along with the flow when a religious topic comes up. But usually, I am looking gracefully for a way to say goodbye and leave because there is no excitement. I know quickly now when I am not speaking with someone who is like-minded in the area of faith. We can be around nice, decent people, but if they have not had a transforming experience, deep down in their hearts, how are they any different from unbelievers in troubling times? Anyone can be nice when they purpose to be. We all can wear a mask when it makes sense to do so.

*"Therefore, I say unto you, Take no thought for your life, What ye shall eat, or what ye shall drink; nor yet for your body, what ye shall put on. Is not the life more than meat, and the body than raiment? Behold the fowls of the air: for they sow not, neither do they reap nor gather into barns; yet our heavenly Father feedeth them. Are yee not much better than they? Which of you by taking thought can add one cubit unto his stature?"~ **Matthew 6: 25-27***

Comment: This passage speaks to the level of trust and belief in God we need to have. That means no worry, doubt, or unbelief. "Take no thought…."

*"Casting all your care upon him; for he careth for you."~ **I Peter 5:7***

Comment: How much should we trust God? Completely: for he cares for us. What are we carrying that we have not cast upon him? Does anything come to mind? Take time to pass that heavy burden to him.

"And when thou prayest, thou shalt not be as the hypocrites are: for they love to pray standing in the synagogues and in the corners of the streets, that they may be seen of men. Verily I say unto you, They have their reward. But thou, when thou prayest, enter into thy closet and when

*thou hast shut thy door, pray to thy Father which is in secret;
and thy Father which seeth in secret shall reward thee
openly. But when ye pray, use not vain repetitions, as the
heathen do: for they think that they shall be heard for their
much speaking. Be not ye therefore like unto them: for your
Father knoweth what things ye have need of, before ye ask
him. After this manner therefore pray ye: Our Father which
art in heaven, Hallowed be thy name. Thy kingdom come. Thy
will be done in earth, as it is in heaven. Give us this day our
daily bread. And forgive us our debts, as we forgive our
debtors. And lead us not into temptation but deliver us from
evil: For thine is the kingdom, and the power, and the glory,
forever. Amen." ~Matthew 6:5-13*

Comment: We are taught here how to pray. Words
from the Master! My assessment of my prayers before I was
born again: many prayers, but often just vain repetition....

*"But seek ye first the kingdom of God, and his
righteousness; and all these things shall be added unto you."
~Matthew 6:33*

Comment: What did I seek first over the course of
my younger years until well into adulthood, when I had my
born-again experience? Honestly, God was not usually the
first in my life. I certainly had been raised to respect God. I
thought going to church on Sunday was what good people do.
I certainly learned to call out to him in times of real need. But
looking back now, it was more like a weekly payment on my
spiritual insurance policy.

*"Ask, and it shall be given you; seek, and ye shall
find, knock, and it shall be opened unto you: For everyone
that asketh receiveth; and he that seeketh findeth, and to him
that knocketh it shall be opened. Or what man is there of you,
whom if his son ask bread, will he give him a stone? Or if he
ask a fish, will he give him a serpent? If ye then, being evil,
know how to give good gifts unto your children, how much*

more shall your Father which is in heaven give good things to them that ask him?" ~**Matthew 7:7-11**

Comment: These are the words of Jesus talking about the compassion and faithfulness of our Heavenly Father.

"In every thing give thanks: for this is the will of God in Christ Jesus concerning you."
~**I Thessalonians 5:18**

Comment: We have every reason because of our God to give thanks in all things. Even when things are going badly, if we truly have faith after sincere prayer, we will know that no matter how it looks at the moment, it will, in the end, turn out good.

"Elias was a man subject to like passions as we are, and he prayed earnestly that it might not rain: and it rained not on the earth by the space of three years and six months."
~**James 5:16**

Comment: If you quoted this to a true environmentalist, it would drive that person nuts. They would never believe God was behind such a verse. Weather extremes do get our attention, don't they? In spite of the weather wars conspiracy, much of it likely true, God is behind it all. I have, at times, prayed concerning the weather and have seen what seemed a miraculous answer. One time it concerned the day of my daughter Mary's wedding. A gloomy, overcast, and very rainy day. Following my prayer, I watched a small batch of blue appear over the church, and there was no rain during the after-wedding courtyard reception. Praise God! He cares for the small things too.

"For the eyes of the Lord are over the righteous, and his ears are open unto their prayers: but the face of the Lord is against them that do evil."
~**I Peter 3:12**

Comment: The God of the Bible takes sides. We all need to know and truly believe this.

"And this is the confidence that we have in him, that, if we ask anything according to his will, he heareth us:" ~*I John 5:14*

Comment: Unbelievers don't often pray, or if they do, it's only in desperation. They don't really believe he hears the prayers of those silly enough to believe in him and pray.

"Likewise, the Spirit also helpeth our infirmities: for we know not what we should pray for as we ought: but the Spirit itself maketh intercession for us with groanings which cannot be uttered." ~*Romans 8:26*

Comment: Praying in the Spirit in an unknown tongue is a powerful tool that I never used in my first forty years. I did not know of this wonderful divine gift as a practicing Roman Catholic. It is not rational for worldly people to believe in such power. One can be worldly and still believe in Jesus Christ. Can you be both worldly and religious? Definitely yes! I now pray daily in my private tongue. I believe strongly in the Holy Ghost.

growing up spiritually

I was born into a family where both my parents grew up going to church on Sundays, My dad continued this practice all his adult life. I certainly heard about the Christian God from the pulpit growing up. Both my parents certainly knew about God. So I did too. My dad was devoted; there were signs he tried to live his life to please God. My mother was more silent concerning her religious beliefs. She was not keen on attending church. I never learned why. Dad was the parent that took us, three boys, to church on Sundays. Mom would stay home, only joining us on Christmas and Easter. She would have a good breakfast or lunch on the table and a clean house when we returned home. Mom was a really good homemaker. She clearly loved all of us and was a stay-at-home mom in the best sense of that phrase. The prayers I experienced growing up were written out ones that I memorized. Although they were excellent prayers and well thought out, they weren't coming straight out of my heart, but my mind: memorized words. Maybe the originator of the prayer had heard from the throne room of God. But it was their honest prayer, not mine. But I certainly prayed many memorized prayers my first 40 years.

real men with real prayers

The first time I ever heard spontaneous praying under the Holy Spirit's inspiration that I remembered was when I joined the Full Gospel Businessmen's Fellowship International in 1978.

I was invited to come to one of their meetings by a new friend I had met upon my return after a year on the island of Okinawa, where I had just had a life-changing encounter with Jesus. I was reassigned to the Seattle, Washington area and met a man, John Andor. He invited me to join this very interesting men's fellowship. This was a group of committed Christian businessmen in the greater Seattle area. Boy, were they on fire for Jesus. I had never met men like this: Don Ostrom, Fred Dorfline, Ed Allen, Bob Bignold, Vince Larson, and many, many others. They and many more had a great influence on my life at a time I needed spiritual mentors. This fellowship group of men was founded by Demos Shakarian, who I met several times. He wrote a great little book called *The Happiest People on Earth*.

As with most man-made works, division eventually crept into this fine group, and it began to splinter into smaller groups with a slightly different focus. This was very unfortunate from my viewpoint. At some point, it was opened up to women during the weekly meetings and not just at the monthly banquets. But for sixteen years during a rocky time in my life before and after an emotional divorce, it provided the Godly fellowship I needed to endure and grow in Christ. This group was a refuge for me during a wilderness time after I retired from active military service but had not settled into a civilian job I really liked. This divorce – not of my own choosing – really threw me into confusion and stress. The Lord, of course, knew what was coming and had prepared others to help me get through this long, difficult, and painful trial. That spiritual transformation while alone in my bedroom eleven years before setting me on a new course and firmly on the narrow path prior to the most difficult challenge of my life. As a result of my full surrender that wonderful night, the Lord worked several miracles. He introduced me to this life-saving fellowship. He brought a few really wonderful Christian brothers into my life to be with me through the difficult times ahead.

Being stationed in Seattle was another miracle. Until my orders were changed, I was slated to become the Recruiting Officer in Kansas City, Missouri. I was not looking forward to that three-year assignment. Suddenly I was headed to the University of Washington, where I had graduated university, to be the Marine Officer Instructor for the NROTC program at the University of Washington (a three-year assignment)!

Once my family was settled in, and work was under control, I started going to an early Thursday morning weekly breakfast meeting at the downtown Seattle Athletic Club. Our family started attending the monthly banquets. There I heard real men pray real prayers. Not the rote ones I had to hear in routine church services all my life and in official ceremonies. These came straight from hearts on fire. They were spot on. Every meeting we saw invited men whose hearts were transformed. Mine included.

My conversion and then joining FGBMFI prepared me for a soon to come very different time in life. Thank God Jesus became real and personal before that storm hit full force. All this impacted my life in ways I could not have anticipated. Things became important to me that were not me before my conversion. My eyes and ears were unplugged spiritually. I saw and heard things in a brand new light.

"Therefore, if any man be in Christ, he is a new creature: old things are passed away; behold, all things are become new." ~**II Corinthians 5:17**

A person physically can look the same and be in most ways that same person after such a life-changing experience. But at the same time, nothing is quite the same anymore. To be born again is to be transformed in thought, word, and deed. A new creation! Of course, there is a lot to learn to understand what has happened to you. And the old nature does not simply go away. It still fights you for control.

My encounter in my room overseas was so unique and different for me, unlike anything that had ever happened before or that I had heard of! I fully shared the experience with no one for some time after it happened. It was so holy and so private. Not even with my wife at that time. Later I told her in bits and pieces. A sane, rational religious intellectual, upon hearing the story, could easily have accused me of losing my mind.

I had grown up in a church that knew a lot about God. It represented itself and still does as the one true church. It was full of rich color, form, ritual, ceremony, and tradition. But it never helped me experience God in such a life-transforming manner. I knew nothing about being born again or being filled with the Spirit or the many ways God communicates with us. I later learned my transforming experience was not unique inside the Catholic Church. Later, I met others after my conversion who had been born again but not inside the church they grew up in. Some stay in the church of their birth for family reasons. Family and friends can be a strong pull on us. But others leave and join a full gospel church that seems more real to them. I tried to stay in and make a difference, but eventually, I felt it was time to leave this institution.

As a practicing Catholic, I believed that a habit of prayer was crucial. I accepted the church's written-out prayers. Many were coming from canonized saints long dead as worth memorizing and repeating often. I thought they all must have had a close relationship with God. I did not understand why he railed against his day's established religion; I never thought about why I was never encouraged to pray from my heart. I had no real understanding of how much God is actually for us and will intervene directly in our affairs. In most Roman Catholic churches I attended, the laity is allowed up near the altar but can only read carefully scripted words. I was a volunteer doing that for years. I never heard actual layperson testimonies from a Roman Catholic pulpit, which is sad. I knew nothing about the many ways we can block our prayers. Yes, we can hinder God's desire to bless us!

Though I thought I knew a lot about the Christian religion, I knew nothing about Protestant beliefs and why the great reformers, all priests, left Roman Catholicism. But the light was switched on around 40, and I began to see things spiritually in a different light. I could say my heart was good toward God as best I knew as a Roman Catholic. I honestly practiced my religion. But I was in a religious tradition that was doing me personally more harm than good, I must say in hindsight. I say this with deep regret.

"For there is one God, and one mediator between God and men, the man Christ Jesus..."
~1 Timothy 2:5

Most Catholics I know are decent, kind people. There are many really lovely people in many religious systems that are just trying to please God. I grew up in one and tried to do the same. After becoming born again and gradually concluding that Roman Catholicism wasn't for me, I spent years exploring the Protestant world, trying to fit in there too. I found that many in the Protestant world are just as held back inside their man-centric systems as I was in the Catholic system. I did find a few churches I would have liked to be a part of but were not close enough to where I worked and lived.

deception a strange blockage

Deception is a strange thing. We can be deceived and really think we know the truth. There are some wonderful people in churches, and they are probably the majority. I just perceived that for many church leaders, it is all about increasing their numbers. I can say that most such institutions have many born-again believers but often are being fed at a lower educational level than what they really need.
~**Hebrews 6: 1-2.**

God knows us from before our births. He knew I was headed toward him even though it was through a maze of confusion. He knew that I would eventually reach my spiritual destination, a full surrender of my life to him. I wasn't under a really dark cloud growing up, just a gray one. During my first 40 years of life, I did learn a lot of Bible truth. I prayed. He often answered my prayers. But I just did not have the discernment and wisdom to see how much better life in Christ could be. I spent too much time trying to reach him through gatherings of people and not enough time trying to reach him in private. I see what is going on now with such clarity. Looking back, I see how his hand was upon me during my journey towards him. But I never saw his grace and favor as I see it now. Earlier in life, I saw a lot of what went on through a belief in luck and chance, though I would not have said it that way. I see now that nothing is by chance. I feel quite alone at times now, but being alone does not bother me the way it used to. I am never really alone as God is with me always. In fact, inside me! And, praise God, I am married to a woman who shares my faith.

the weapons of our warfare

Strong faith and effective communication are vital parts of successful warfare. In the church, a person is involved with a scale of bad to good, which can hinder or help one's ability to communicate with God. Not all religious organizations are equal. I am at the age where my wife and I both have a strong relationship with God. We have a church in our home, the two of us, daily. But *"we don't neglect the fellowship of the saints"* meeting often with others of like mind. Jesus is faithful to show up when we join hands to pray or study the Bible or worship or just discuss spiritual matters. I know this because we can feel his presence and the anointing. I love his promise to be where two or three gather in his name. I love the phrase in the subtitle above. It speaks to me. That is why I highlighted this particular verse, **II Corinthians 10:4**, in the book's front. When a real believer starts praying, the angels of God start moving to respond. I love what **Deuteronomy 9:3** says:

"Understand therefore this day, that the LORD thy God is he which goeth over before thee; As a consuming fire he shall destroy them, and he shall bring them down before thy face: so shalt thou drive them out, and destroy them quickly, as the LORD hath said unto thee."

When in the right relationship, God is the one who goes out and fights for us. What a great God we serve! I am so thankful I live in the New Testament period rather than back before the first coming of Jesus Christ. Our relationship with God is so much more personal. The veil has been torn in two. We do not need a human priest or pastor to approach him for us. I am so thankful we have only one mediator, and his name is Jesus. The phrase *"consuming fire"* is found thirty-three times in my Bible. I love that this concept of God and his awesome power is repeated in the New Testament for us who believe in Jesus.

"For our God is a consuming fire."~ **Hebrews 12:29**

With such a powerful God, we must communicate properly with him in faith to fight for us. There is so much power available to us when we are in the right relationship with God. One of my favorite verses is in **Luke**.

"Behold, I give unto you power to tread on serpents and scorpions, and over all the power of the enemy: and nothing shall by any means hurt you. "~Luke 10:19

A lot of things hold us back from reaching our full potential in life. For me, in the first 40 years, the thing that held me back the most was not knowing God's word. I was reading out of the **Psalms** recently. I try to read one chapter of **Proverbs** and five chapters of **Psalms** daily in the morning to Karen as she is in the kitchen. I read this passage. It impacted me, so I will share it in closing this chapter.

"When wisdom entereth into thine heart, and knowledge is pleasant unto thy soul; Discretion shall preserve thee, understanding shall keep thee: To deliver thee from the way of the evil man, from the man that speaketh froward things; Who leave the paths of uprightness, to walk in the ways of darkness; Who rejoice to do evil, and delight in the forwardness of the wicked; Whose ways are crooked, and they froward in their paths:" ~**Proverbs 2:10-15**

When a man or woman makes the decision to make the written word of God, his daily companion, communication with God comes alive in a brand-new way. It really did for me after 40 years of trying it the religious way. I really can't read his word without my spirit being quickened to write down a verse or passage. That very verse often helps me that very day, or someone I share it with really needs to hear that verse. Do you want to be used more by God? Read his word more diligently. It will motivate you, and you will, in turn, often get to share it with others. And it will boost both your faith and the one you share with.

10

THE FEAR of DYING

Those who enlist know that they are given an insurance policy upon being ordered overseas, make out a will and settle their civilian affairs before saying goodby to loved ones and friends to depart for their overseas assignment.

I am not aware Herman Cain ever had military experience. But he had a militant persona. He was a political figure who seemed not to fear man. He died July 30, 2020, supposedly of Covid-19. This surprises me as he was a man of God for sure. His death at 74 makes me very sad. His funeral was not; I expect as crowded as another black man's funeral, John Lewis. He died just after him, John Lewis. He, too, seemed to be a decent man, but he was more politically correct in the elite's eyes, for he was a lifelong democrat. Herman Cain left the democratic plantation for conservatism and never looked back. For that reason, most liberals hated him. He was not afraid to speak the truth. I do not know what the real cause of death was, probably some underlying medical condition. He would be sad that they are saying he died from this flu going around that is being used, I think, to bring in the one-world government. I hate the fear I see concerning this flu. Such a spirit of fear! I am praying that people will wake up and see it for what it is. An attempt to scare people into going along with the political agenda of Bill Gates! Population reduction!

Fear of death is at the top of most people's list of fears. Except for the young and foolish! Many of them do not seem to understand how fragile life can be. Many young Americans have not had much experience struggling out on their own. We do see a spike in suicides among the young. And those whites who join Antifa will find that life will not go well for them! Taking calculated risks is a part of decision-making, but they are making terrible decisions. Such risks can land these radicals in hell. Taking another's life has terrible eternal consequences! Joining Antifa is not rational!

No matter how bad life is at the moment, there should be hope for positive change. Most decisions people make do not result in a quick death. But such choices are on the increase in the terminal generation. Crazy people seem to be the fastest expanding group across America. For them, the status quo must be unbearable. But thinking the same way as before, which has not worked, is not likely to lead to anyone's breakthrough. Why is finding Jesus Christ and surrendering one's life to him such a hard thing to do?

This generation has been hyped as the smartest people alive. Yet, they summarily reject the one who died for them so that they could truly live. Why such stubbornness against the gospel? The answer is that the devil is real and knows his time is short.

On a risk scale of one to ten, those who are super cautious and unhappy seem less likely to make any drastic change in their basic life assumption. Assumptions are the foundation of all decision-making. Because God has been removed from all secular education, many young people are blind to spiritual reality, which is very sad. That is why sharing the gospel when prompted to do so is very important. Many millennials are flying blind. Thank goodness God has created enough open-minded people who are looking for ways to explain the growing craziness, open to exploring other explanations of the truth, and are open to honest debate. History records how perishable societies are. Fear of death should have little to do with our life decisions. The young and healthy frankly should believe they will live a long, productive life. It is a sad thing to believe you will die before your time.

morbid thoughts

For me, morbid thoughts like I could die if I take this risk were not a part of my thought life growing up. I am not a reckless person by nature. Deep down, I just trusted I would not die when taking a calculated risk. I expected everything would work out for me. How some think is quite different from what my thought patterns were in the 1950-the 60s.

We find the word, *die,* 518 times, and *death* 410 times in God's word. The process of *dying* is not something men usually think about. But if your thinking trends toward worst case thinking, such as death, a great place to explore this subject is to read the Bible seriously. Early death is undoubtedly a subject worth exploring especially if you or someone you know is in a situation where that is more than a remote possibility. Who has not had a scary dream where death pursued him, and he woke up sweating profusely? Or a close call while driving avoiding an almost fatal accident! Such an experience can cause flashbacks and lead to panic attacks.

The Bible faces this topic head-on. Most healthy young people expect death to pass them by. The bullet is meant for someone else. Most of us do not dwell much on such morbid possibilities. Yet we see that suicide among the young is now at an all-time high. Why so? I think because fewer people are putting their life in the hands of God.

Suicide is only spoken of twice in the Bible, the suicide of King Saul. Saul was not afraid to die. Why did he take his own life? It seems to prevent his enemy from capturing him alive and the humiliation that would follow. He killed himself to deprive his enemies of the pleasure of killing him. It seems a perverse form of pride to see suicide as an honorable action. It certainly demonstrates a lack of trust in God's saving power. In the Bible, we know that it is human nature to fight to hang on to one's life. God makes this instinct very strong in all of us. Few want to die. God is the author of life.

killing zones

The young are being indoctrinated against anything associated with guns in our society, except, of course, inside the gang cultures. Satan is the master of the takeover. He doesn't want us to be able to defend ourselves. No one is better than Satan at taking over all secular institutions and organizations across all societies and nations. He then turns them into vehicles to control others in an unholy way. Evil governments have proven to be the most effective killing machines across history. American schools and hospitals all got their start as good Christian works. They have mostly been taken over by non-Christians and are managed as secular institutions where God is no longer welcome. Look what is happening on school properties that are gun-free zones—an increase in mass shootings. Look at what is happening inside hospitals: a rise in hospital-related deaths. Poor doctoring is now the third leading cause of all deaths. Bad people are adept at the strategy of hostile takeovers.

The main thing we are told that stands between governments and the citizens when evil prevails are guns in the hands of the righteous. Take them away, and you see by studying history that the biggest serial killers are governments. Not the occasional lone fanatic! Out of control governments are the reason for our 2nd Amendment to our U. S. Constitution! One must wonder if many serial killings could have been stopped but were not to create public fear for the purpose of disarming the populous. Some call such operations false flag events. In addition to guns in the hands of the righteous, there is another even more effective weapon. But it is not talked about in the public arena because it is no longer politically correct. What is this weapon? The power of prayer.

That is why it will be so devastating to the righteous who are not Christians when the rapture happens. They will be left behind in a culture of death when God's praying people have been removed. What terror that sudden realization will be! They will want to die. Many will choose martyrdom rather than take the mark of the beast.

Many of those who control our current American cities are trying to emotionally and mentally neuter boys before becoming men. Last week, a national story about a schoolgirl who was arrested for pointing her index finger and pretending to shoot a classmate. Usually, it is boys that are prone to such actions. Calling the police to deal with such a bogus threat is insane. A form of school indoctrination gone amuck! We are now living in a full-blown mommy-dominated society.

In Vietnam, in late 1964, I experienced my first enemy "killing zone." It was during an operation with the 2nd battalion, Vietnamese Marines. When I later entered Vietnam that following Spring as a part of the Marine Brigade out of Hawaii, we had backup navy assets that gave me great comfort. Much of Vietnam from the news seemed to be laced with such killing zones.

confidence builders

First, I think of the naval medical assistance that supports all Marine infantry units! At the squad level attached to all infantry companies, we have a corpsmen team. They are highly trained in how to give life support to those who are seriously wounded. These first aid providers at the scene of all firefights are backed up by a rapid response evacuation system from the rear area forward to support the medical responders at the edge of and into the battle areas. We Marines love our corpsman.

When we engaged with the enemy, helicopters in the air could come into where we were to evacuate our seriously wounded in minutes. This system was not possible before the Korean War. I remember one instance when I had to evacuate my artillery forward observer, an officer assigned to me for that particular operation. He was seriously wounded.

We had discovered within 1200 yards of Vandegrift Combat Base, in very rugged terrain on the reverse side of a ridgeline that could easily be seen from Vandegrift Combat Base, a dug into the backside of the ridgeline, living area for enemy troops. They directed the firing of rockets toward our line of bases. While I was out on a three-day patrol with my rifle company, we discovered the edge of this complex late in the afternoon. At about 2300 that night, our perimeter was attacked. It was a considerable force. We called in artillery fire from Vandegrift Combat Base during the fight. My forward observer was hit by incoming fire and wounded badly enough we called for a medical evac right away. It was necessary to save his life. Time was of the essence. Unfortunately, he died later in triage after he was successfully extracted.

There were very tall trees in the area. We discovered a small clearing where we could see the stars. We marked the small opening with flares so the inbound chopper could find the opening. A firefight was going on in the dark. They lowered a bucket bed. He was hosted up about 150 feet to the hovering helicopter. This was only a hundred yards to the rear of where our forward platoon was engaged with the enemy. It was a very dark night and during the rainy season. The day before our discovery, it had rained so hard that for 24 hours, we had to hole up and wait out the rain. It had become too difficult to move. I heard later that 26 inches of rain fell that particular day.

It was the next day after the nighttime engagement that we discovered the huge underground complex. The enemy started this firefight as a distraction to evacuate their underground facility.

Most Marines, unless they get into fear and depression, usually due to other personal problems (often ones back home), do not dwell on death. Marines love the corpsmen who accompany our fighting units. For the most part, they act like the heroes they are during such enemy actions. They put themselves in harm's way to help the ones doing the fighting.

We need the second naval asset the chaplains assigned to each infantry battalion, regiment, and division. These men and their assistants attempt to take care of our spiritual needs. Before the start of any operation, they make themselves available for counseling and spiritual services. We are spiritual beings who have a body. Before exposure to firefights and possible death, men need to be allowed to repent, forgive, and confess Christ. They need to know they can stand clean before God and that a besetting sin will not take them to hell if killed.

They need to understand that death is not the worst thing that can happen to them. That heaven is a real place! There is what is known as the *"second death,"* which is far worse and not to be compared with normal death. It is the chaplains who should have the knowledge to discuss such matters and bring them comfort. Before discussing the second death more thoroughly, I want to mention the three other wonderful naval assets that help Marines to bring the terror of death to the other side in a fight.

Naval gunfire from an offshore ship's weapons system and naval aircraft overhead when we were operating near the sea gives us the added firepower needed to bring instant fear to the enemy. And, of course, it took the logistical support from the navy to get us to the fight, land us, and keep the supplies coming in during the fight. Marines look to and appreciate our navy counterparts. They are absolutely essential in projecting America's military might into the camp of the enemy when necessary. Sometimes it's the Army backing us up. They do a wonderful job also when we needed resources not organic to the Marines.

a fate worse than death

"He that hath an ear let him hear what the Spirit saith unto the churches; He that overcometh shall not be hurt of the second death."
~ *Revelation 2:11*

During my years in the Marines, I never knew or was told about the second death. **Revelation's book** talks about the second death in four different verses: the one above and **Revelation 20:6, 14, and 21:8**. Nowhere else is this particular phrase found. This is crucial information for someone threatened with dying to know. From a spiritual standpoint, I see two types of warfighters. Those who are on the broad path (**Matthew 7:13-14**) headed toward hell, and those who have chosen the narrow way. The wise overcomer has surrendered his life to Christ and is on the path toward heaven. Many of those I fought within Vietnam, I do not think, had a deep understanding of the spiritual consequences of dying. Most were good Marines. There is a growing number in these times who serve in our armed forces who do not have a Christian worldview. May God bless them for their willingness to put themselves in harm's way. There is a great mission field within the armed forces. Believers who enlist should see themselves as ambassadors of Christ.

We are blessed with salvation and should want to share it wherever possible. I am not advocating being pushy. That comes across as religious pride. But bold where the opportunity opens naturally to talk about the gospel of salvation.

If asked by a religious person for one good reason why any believer should enlist in the United States' armed forces, my answer would be because it is a great field full of lost souls. Many mission fields are less dangerous. For certain people, God does call into the uniformed services to show the light of Christ to that part of the fallen world. God wishes that none should perish. He sends his kingdom ambassadors everywhere, even into harm's way.

"And he said unto them, Go ye into all the world and preach the gospel to every creature."
~Mark 16:18

Some men who are exposed to death on a routine basis have a tendency to exhibit a lot of "brave talk." Quite frankly, many of these sorts are open to hearing the gospel presented to them at that time. With death staring us in the face, only fools would have a closed mind at that time. The same men might never be open during more normal times. It is like going into open-heart surgery where the odds are not in your favor: wouldn't you be grateful if someone asked you if you feared death, listened to your answer, and then appropriately shared why you shouldn't be afraid to die? Common sense would tell most to prepare their hearts just in case, wouldn't you think. I did talk with an acquaintance who was a confessing atheist a few years ago. He was scheduled for open-heart surgery. Sadly, he was hardened against the gospel. He shut me down when I tried to share. He was a fellow Vietnam Vet but was not open. This surprised me. He is a nice guy, but a confirmed agnostic. He did live and is still not open. These are serious times. God provides us all opportunities to speak on his behalf. Do not miss these important opportunities.

"Whosoever, therefore, shall be ashamed of me and of my words in this adulterous and sinful generation; of him also shall the Son of man be ashamed, when he cometh in the glory of his Father with the holy angels." ~**Mark 8:38**

Frankly, when we look at all the Christians killed because of their faith over the past 2,000 years: it is often not easy to share the gospel. There are risks. In America, political correctness has made it more costly. Christians have lost their jobs in recent years for this reason. We see cake bakers sued by gays because their conscience does not permit them to cater to such events. I am sure believers have been killed here in America for their faith. It just happened in Portland, and the Antifa thug was later caught and killed. Liberal politicians have opened the doors to such violence. But it is not yet like it is in many Muslim-controlled nations. Thank God!

"And death and hell were cast into the lake of fire. This is <u>the second death</u>" ~**Revelation 20:14**

"But the fearful, and unbelieving, and the abominable, and murders, and whoremongers, and sorcerers, and idolaters, and all liars, shall have their part in the lake which burneth with fire and brimstone: which is <u>the second death.</u>" ~**Revelation 21:8**

Where will a non-Christian hear the gospel if they will not approach a chaplain or someone they know who is a believer? God always has someone who knows the truth living amongst unbelievers. When could a nonbeliever be more open to hearing the gospel than when beside such a believer, both facing a common danger? Many who are in the armed forces for enlistment are never really exposed to much danger at all. Does that explain why some live like they are anxious to go to hell? Things can change so quickly even they might be open to being evangelized. Thank God there are praying parents and grandparents whose prayers follow such family members around. Many of us will only find out how much their prayers keep us going and alive when we reach heaven.

Risks are taken on the obstacle course and other hardening training designed to get one past certain basic fear, and the normal moral risks while on liberty are the scariest times many who enlist will ever face. Everyone who enlists is exposed to a class taught by the chaplain's service. Everyone knows where to go for spiritual help officially. I have met many who were exposed to Christ at the family level or briefly through friends or from a message heard on the radio. Men are without excuse who reach hell. Still, it amazes me how many are hardened and inoculated against the gospel.

doomed

I am a confirmed believer. I have been given spiritual gifts. I have some discernment. I would not say I am a perceiver. I am married to one with that gift for sure, my wife. She perceives things I miss concerning matters of the heart. Sometimes I too have clues about such attitudes. But I can smell danger in a way most civilians who have not had their skills exercised by combat cannot. I had smelled death on people before it happened. Some do have a premonition when they are dangerously at risk. Still, many do not have any desire to hear the gospel! They have no inkling how much they need to hear and accept the salvation message. I can perceive when I have no opening to share with such souls. Many times, I have no unction to pray for such people. Why is that? Have they burned through their last opportunity? Are there people who are really doomed to hell for all eternity? Some people speak death: others life. Scripture tells us:

*"Death and life are in the power of the tongue: and they that love it shall eat the fruit thereof." ~**Proverbs 18:21***

blasphemy

If a person burns through every righteous person God has placed across his or her ordained path where such a person will hear God's truth, God then has no one else to work with to save a person. Would God then have to abandon him? Only God knows the answer. Can sociopaths ever be saved? Research tells us they have no compassion for others. Are such people doomed to hell at birth? How about narcissists? There is free will. These are difficult questions. I had in earlier times assumed that all could be saved until the moment of death. I now think otherwise. I think people can go too far. Just today, I got an urge to study the word "blaspheme." I find it used 54 times in the King James Bible. A lot of people who do not know God are blasphemers. You hear them all the time. They seem to have no care for who overhears them. Can they be saved? Some for sure. But there is one category that cannot be saved according to scripture—those who blaspheme the Holy Spirit.

"Wherefore I say unto you, All manner of sin and blasphemy shall be forgiven unto men: but the blasphemy against the Holy Ghost shall not be forgiven unto men."~ ***Matthew 12:31***

This doctrine is reiterated in **Mark 3:29** and in **Luke 12:10**. The Father has sent the Holy Ghost to believers, knowing their need for divine help because of evil's growing power. We desperately need this help. It is why The Father sent this help, so we could overcome all evil. Behind evil stands a supernatural force. It must be overcome by divine power. To blaspheme such help is the unforgivable sin. If you have the Holy Ghost inside you, it makes sense that those who are possessed by evil would recognize you. The spirit inside them can see your strong spirit, and so takes an instant disliking to you. Have you tried to be nice to someone, and no matter what you do, it does not overcome their dislike? They are cold as ice toward your attempts to befriend them. Could it be they are rejecting the Holy Spirit inside you?

There is much division in the church over what the gifts of the Holy Spirit are. Some gifts are not welcomed in some churches. Tongues, for example! They are seen as gifts of the devil. Be very careful in what you come to believe concerning the gifts of the Holy Spirit. They are spelled out very clearly in **1 Corthinians 12 and 14** and elsewhere. There is not much teaching from these chapters from most pulpits where I have been a member or attended. It seems many pastors stay away from anything too controversial. By avoiding such passages, the saints are not fully equipped for the work of the ministry.

Those of us who believe and have accepted the atoning work of the cross and are looking to Jesus receive supernatural giftings. Some operational, but much more inactive because of fear of man. Brothers who study scripture should not let differing opinions over what a verse might be saying divide them when it comes to facing the common enemy, Satan.

dying to self

When an individual becomes part of the armed forces, he is sworn in. He takes an oath to defend the Constitution against all enemies, both foreign and domestic. All armed forces personnel take an oath of enlistment. This differentiates our work from most civilians who never take an official oath as a civilian except maybe for jury duty. These are solemn moments. The idea crosses some of our minds that the carrying out of this oath could be costly. We see this costly sacrifice in many of the living veterans who once served. It can require life or limb. The duty of a soldier is all about defending life, not taking lives. Yes, it might require one to kill. That is a consequence of our being a defender and being under lawful authority.

Killing is different than murder. Our nation has not been about the conquest of other nations since the Indian Wars. It is about the defense of this nation and our key allies.

In preparing to accomplish our particular duties as a part of the armed forces, we are disciplined. Our training requires us to become tougher physically, emotionally, mentally, and spiritually than those we meet in combat. The Marine Corp's leadership paragraph of the governing manual of policies and procedures says this:

"Because those who enlist are in the formative years of their lives that we owe it to their parents and the nation that upon their discharge from service they are far better off mentally, physically and morally than when they first enlisted."

These words were penned by General John L. Lejeune, who was the Commandant of Marines in the 1920s. He started the leadership training program. He was a man's man, and his memory is revered among Marines. He saw Marines as a precious national asset. The death of even one Marine he thought should be taken very seriously.

the army of the Lord

When you surrender your life and join the army of the LORD like in any army, the general or admiral requires discipline in his command. We need to bring our flesh into submission! We are disciplined for our own good. We are hardened to become more effective. We will never amount to much as a Christian if our spirit does not rule over our flesh. The flesh does not want to die. Even a physical army requires this. When your flesh rules, the general direction it heads in is toward hell. It wants its own way. Always! But you have a general who has pledged to protect you, who loves you.

Look around this world. Watch the many people who have no control over their appetites, supersizing past the point of obesity—becoming instant candidates for diabetes, heart attacks, and strokes! Many walk the streets addicted to drugs and alcohol. This is not normal. Many more are unhappy, blaming others for their unhappiness but rarely taking personal responsibility for their dysfunctional actions. Some of this behavior is because of real disabilities, not of their own making. Yes! These people do need serious help. But a lot of medical problems are due to poor judgment and decision making, bordering on rebellion.

Discipline is at the core of good living. Without a combination of discipline, internal and external, how can an organization or the larger society stay on an even keel? A lack of discipline leads to breakdowns and chaos. If a person is not willing to discipline himself, he must be disciplined by others.

When my dad was chief of staff of Parris Island, South Carolina, the Marine Corps East Coast boot camp, it was my senior year of high school. I remember letters from grateful parents written to the Commanding General of the base, thanking them for what they had done for their sons. Dad would sometimes bring a copy of such a letter home to read at the dinner table. Parents could not believe the positive changes and were so appreciative. The external discipline and quality leadership and the young men's supervised effort led to very real personal transformations. It astonished many parents. Discipline does wonders. But at the other extreme, the McKein Incident was resulting in a trial to convict a Sergeant who took his recruit platoon on an unauthorized night march, and some drowned. In the age we are in, the growing lack of discipline is so transforming our nation to march in the wrong direction. At the heart of this hatred of discipline is the antichrist spirit. We do have a president who has been in office over three years, as I type this, who is trying to "Make America Great Again." He seems to be a modern-day Cyrus. A gift from God to America and the world. He is reversing many of the negative trends by the power of quality leadership. But there is so much to be turned around. And so many in places of power are fighting him tooth and nail. Who will win this power struggle?

a house divided

A house divided cannot stand. I heard Rush Limbaugh say that there were seven million unfilled jobs, indicating we are at full employment. As I review this draft, Covid-19 has seriously wounded our economy, and we are no longer at or near full employment. Can our President turn things around once again? A segment of our population is working hard to ensure that does not happen.... Donald Trump is a very talented man, but he won't be able to do it without God's help. Covid-19, though certainly a plan of the Deep State, appears to be an act of God. We certainly are a deeply divided nation.

*"And Jesus knew their thought, and said unto them, every kingdom divided against itself is brought to desolation; and every city or house divided against itself shall not stand:"~ **Matthew12:25***

Will our nation be counted at the judgment among the sheep or the goat nations? The prayers and actions of the saints of God will determine the answer. The most powerful prayers come from those who have put their flesh to death. They are the ones who have divine protection and do not fear death. A minimal number compared with all who are members of an established Christian body.

there is a generation

Does God talk about the terminal generation in scripture? There is a passage in the book of Proverbs I find very interesting in this regard.

"There is a generation that curse their father, and doth not bless their mother. There is a generation that are pure in their own eyes, and yet is not washed from their filthiness. There is a generation, O how lofty are their eyes! and their eyelids are lifted up. There is a generation, whose teeth are as swords, and their jaw teeth as knives, to devour the poor from off the earth, and the needy from among

men...The eye that mocketh at his father, and despiseth to obey his mother, the ravens of the valley shall pick it out, and the young eagles shall eat it. " ~**Proverbs 30: 11-14, 17**

Could it be that this above passage is referring to the Millennials? This is a well-studied generation. Is this what is being said about many in this particular generation? Is this passage referring to them? A significant number of them have not died to self. Many have turned their backs on the God of the Bible. Many in Antifa and BLM are from their ranks. They could easily be the ones to betray the values of our forefathers who established this nation. Many who signed the Declaration of Independence sacrificed their lives and their fortunes. Many in this grouping of Americans need our prayers. Where they go in the next few years could go our nation. Our nation hangs in the balance.

Many millennials are wonderful young adults and do not deserve what is being said about them and their peers. Unfortunately, this passage does apply to a significant number in that generation who are self-absorbed, ungrateful and have huge, unrealistic expectations. They could be the Benedict Arnolds who will betray our nation in this age we live in.

When I look at the grandchildren in Karen and my extended family, I am very hopeful. Though a few were double-minded, the majority of our seventeen grandchildren are pointed toward God. But it is up to the church to get into prayer and make sure that the great majority of these undecided millennials and even those who have headed away from Jesus Christ will do a turnaround.

"If my people, which are called by my name, shall humble themselves, and pray, and seek my face, and turn from their wicked ways; then will I hear from heaven, and will forgive their sin, and will heal their land." ~ **II Chronicals 7:14**

11

BETRAYAL

In Vietnam, it was not easy knowing who your enemies were. Who would betray you? When the 1ˢᵗ Marine Brigade out of Hawaii was committed to the fight and landed in the Chu Lai area in May of 1965, we had prepared for opposition to the landing. The day before the operation was launched, word came down it would be an administrative landing. So, ours was a peaceful entry into Vietnam.

We went ashore, established our positions, set up our perimeters, and settled in to await further orders. The officials in the vicinity welcomed us and used the occasion where possible to do business. They offered various services for profit like barber shops, laundry services, selling cokes, baked bread, etc. Services those in the forward-deployed rifle companies could pay for and might want to take advantage of. Later I heard some started offering services in the dark: drugs, alcohol, and prostitution. Some will do anything to make a profit. We helped their economy by purchasing products and services. Among the locals that came and went, spies were spying out our weaknesses before an upcoming attack. We routinely began short patrols beyond our perimeters. Soon we began encountering the occasional sniper and booby trap. The fight ratcheted up slowly at first.

We gathered intelligence on the enemy's activities. There was the occasional foray into an identified enemy stronghold. What most surprised me was the friendly civilian barber by day who later killed, attacking a rear area during the night. We trusted the friendly faces giving us a shave and haircut. We came to help them. How could they betray us? We were not there to take advantage of them. Such betrayals were difficult. We tried to treat the civilians as friends.

As a Marine, my training was designed to identify and defend myself against uniformed enemies. What shocked me most during the years of the war in Vietnam? Not the enemies of South Vietnam, but Americans stateside who actively turned against our efforts to stop communism's advance. The liberal media and such got away with real verbal murder with their war of words. Their stateside anti-war activities took their toll. Not just on our morale, but in seeding doubt about what kind of men we who served really were. They accused us of being baby killers! And the wisdom of the whole reason for being there! Their stateside behavior reinforced the will of our enemy overseas. The primary reason the war was lost was our stateside betrayal. Then there was the sad aftermath: P.T.S.D. Issues proliferated following the Vietnam War. Many discharged veterans were treated horribly upon our return. Some former friends did not take our side, not wanting to identify actively with those of us who served honorably. Not willing to offend our accusers!

an oath to defend

I had taken an oath to defend the U.S. Constitution against all enemies, both foreign and domestic. Our domestic enemies became obvious over time. The Press was identifying themselves as a major foe of the truth! Sadly, many in the general public bought into their lies over time. In fact, the benefit of the doubt was given far more to the anti-war faction than to those who served.

wasting the early years

Looking at young people today, there are many who are really trying to cooperate with their teachers and make their parents proud during their school years. Thank God for such young people. It is those who the weight of responsibility must sooner rather than later fall upon. I am writing now from the vantage point of eighty-two years of age. My natural hair color has faded into gray and white. Our grandchildren are all millennials except for one. These millennials, over 80 million, are the largest sector of our population of 350 million now. Karen and I have a growing number of great-grandchildren.

God has given me a heart not just for our youth but in particular for struggling millennials, of which much has been written. Up to 40% of that group of young people it is said are by all measures struggling as no generation before. Who is to blame for their condition? That answer is up for grabs. At some point, the blame will fall on their shoulders entirely. One of the essential leadership principles is to accept responsibility and take responsibility for one's actions and the situation. Researchers right now are placing more blame on their parents. They have a name for those parents who still have an adult child living at home. Helicopter parents! They still hover over their now-grown children. Worried about their future, they still try to over supervise them.

Ask any Marine of any generation. He will tell you that the number one complaint Marines have about leadership is over supervision. No one likes to be hovered over, unaware of the undertones of growing anger towards their parents. But I blame the deep state who has taken over large parts of our society and turned against the family using the educations system and other institutions to attack the righteous.

I was taught how to take on overseas enemies. I was not taught what to do about those stateside who hated and mistreated us. We must be under a legal chain of command when confronting our domestic enemies. Many who protested violently, and many more behind the scenes, such as supporters in the mass media, education system, and elsewhere, need right now to be confronted. They weren't years ago but thank God we have President Trump, who never fails to call them the fake media. But the blindness, stubbornness, double-mindedness, and real evil he is encountering is terrible. He needs prayer. Many in the church sleep on, oblivious to what is really going on.

How does one handle one on one encounters with disturbed citizens sympathetic to the enemy? They are hostile to those of us carrying out official U. S. policies. They have closed minds. They cannot be confronted in love and with honest dialog! That just leaves travelling prayer, letters to the editor, and appeals to Congress for millions of citizens who see what is happening. Many do not know what to do about this growing divisiveness, so turn a blind eye. How many are praying effectively? Would things be turning around if that were the case? It is the uncaring attitudes I sense that concern me.

Decades after we had entered Vietnam, they (the ungodly inside America), not those we fought overseas against, had carried the day. We abandoned South Vietnam to the communists because of the rebellion back home within our national ranks. And they are still amongst us and have not repented.

The aftermath of that defeat for me was that I had to watch people like John Kerry and Jane Fonda, traitors in my view, gain more power and influence. Real traitors they were! Both have continued to do real damage in the aftermath of that unpopular war. It was awful. Lies, lies, and more lies they told. America, over time, has become more a culture of lies than the truth in many ways. But the worst was those who had been sent to Vietnam who served honorably and later took their own lives in deep despair. Victims of wicked treachery. During the past fifty years, as I have voted and watched the national scene more and more, I am aware of a kingdom struggle. When you look at the 53 times, the word betrayal is used; that is what a Bible study of this word shows, a spiritual and earthly kingdom struggle of good against evil.

Except for the years of President Reagan's presidency (1981 – 1989), to be frank, until Donald Trump came along, we have been giving ground to these leftist, communist, anti-God forces inside our nation. The avalanche of bad changes started with our withdrawal from Vietnam. I had some hope when the two Bushes were elected, but both of them largely disappointed me. In hindsight, it seems they, too, were part of the deep state. I loved President Reagan. But until President Trump, it has been mostly a downward slide for America toward the abys.

the enemy within

My wife, Karen, had an interesting short prophetic vision she shared with me a decade ago. *On his back, she saw on the ground with one knee bent, looking up, a very strong, powerful warrior in Roman garb. He had a shield in his left hand and a sword in his right, looking up from the ground at something with a terrified look. She thought: who put down such a powerful man? My wife pondered this thought. Then she followed his gaze upward to see a mirror suspended in the sky with his reflection in it. The lesson! We are our own worst enemies.*

My active-duty time as a Marine was essentially about building character into me to make me be the best I could be for our nation and my family. First, military training focused on us as individuals. As I think about our training; so much of it early on was about personal transformation mentally, physically, emotionally, and hopefully morally.

One of the many things an officer learns in his leadership training is *"trust but verify."* How can we ever trust others if we are not trustworthy ourselves? Meaning full of integrity! A major leadership principle is to set an example. It is human nature to have self-doubt as we grow toward manhood. Will we measure up? Can we be counted upon by others in the face of hardship and difficulty? Can we look at death in the face and carry out our duties? These are tough questions. If we want to succeed in life, we must ask ourselves tough questions. And we must be able to do this nationally, too, if we are to survive as a nation. I do not see a fair press anymore. Surveys show 9 of 10 reporters vote democrat. Where's the balance? Political correctness is certainly a tool of the anti-christ.

There are no real shortcuts in life unless you go along with evil. They do give an unfair advantage to their advocates. Many behave as if there are honest shortcuts. Many will lie to themselves and engage in cheating and deceiving others. For many in Antifa and BLM, they are being paid to do what they are doing. For a while, they may fool themselves and others. But such behaviors all come crashing down at some point for those who venture down that deceptive trail full of lies and self-imposed blindness. This seems to be where we are as a nation—divided by a lying spirit! Brother against brother.

decision to retire

I clearly remember the day I decided to retire from military service. It was a Sunday morning. I was in Mill Creek, Washington, in my home, reading the Everett Herald newspaper. There was a four-page section on what had happened since the U.S. withdrawal from Vietnam.

Pictured was the final withdrawal from the tall American embassy building in Saigon. A helicopter was on the roof, with a full load of people with more people trying to board. It was a desperate, chaotic moment. That article had two sentences that changed my direction in life. I had a paradigm shift in understanding. For the first time, I realized we were in a spiritual battle. I had spent years of my life focusing on the possibility of future physical combat with a national enemy while largely ignoring the spiritual battle Satan was engaged in against individuals inside our nation. The clarity at that moment! Who the main enemy really was crystalized for me. I promised God my focus would forever change.

Many of those I had served with in Vietnam upon their return came back to a nation that turned their back on them. They were isolated and rejected. In growing desperation, some took their own lives by suicide. Others by steering their car off the road into a tree at 80 miles an hour! Neither is normal behavior. Wives met many men at the front door with divorce papers in their hands. 36%! This was the first time I became aware of P.T.S.D. Another destroyer of lives! I was nine months from coming into the zone for promotion to full colonel when I retired to fight in a different way, spiritually.

Up to that moment, I had felt called by God to military life. A short time after reading those awful statistics I put in for retirement to get involved in the lesser-known fight ongoing across the earth: Satan's war: to kill, capture, and destroy! I began to study this spiritual war. I really knew very little about anything at that point from a religious perspective. The only thing I now saw clearly was who the real enemy really was. In the natural, it did not seem wise to retire from military service at this time. I had a lot going for me. I was sure I would have been promoted. Retiring to become a civilian writer and speaking about spiritual warfare was a step into the unknown. I sensed it would not be easy. And it wasn't! But it proved to be a real step toward Christ and a deeper relationship with him.

a house divided

*" And one shall say unto him, What are these wounds in thine hands? Then he shall answer, Those with which I was wounded in the house of my friends. " **Zechariah 13: 6***

I was not raised up in a home where my father and mother argued. If they ever did, they had the good sense not to do it in front of their three boys. From my freshman year at the University of Washington until graduation four years later, I was under contract to the military studying to become a future military officer. Once commissioned I served 21 years on active duty. After retirement, I was subject to recall to active service for another nine years as a regular officer.

During all those years, some of my focus was on keeping physically fit if called back to help defend my country. We had a forward-deployed strategy to fight in our enemy's backyard rather than ours. Since retiring in 1983, I have seen increasing division across our land, at the family, community, state, and national level. Creating division is one of Satan's greatest tactics. I would say his main strategy is to lie about most everything. Jesus has told us he is the father of lies. The military is careful to present a united front. After all, military leaders for the common good must work with both republicans and democrats who can have sharp differences of opinion. Few outsiders catch a good Marine bad-mouthing another Marine. Each of us has strong opinions, but the true professional keeps divisive thoughts to himself. There might be one or two he can share privately without it getting back to the wrong person, but they are rare. When the chips are down, even marines we are not personally drawn to will be there for us against the greater enemy.

"And Jesus knew their thoughts, and said unto them, Every kingdom divided against itself is brought to desolation;

*and every city or house divided against itself shall not stand:
And if Satan cast out Satan, he is divided against himself;
how shall then his kingdom stand? And if I by Beelzebub cast
out devils, by whom do your children cast them out?
Therefore they shall be your judges. But if I cast out devils by
the Spirit of God, then the kingdom of God is come unto you.
Or else how can one enter into a strong man's house, and
spoil his goods, except he first bind the strong man? And then
he will spoil his house. He that is not with me is against me.
And he that gathereth not with me scattereth abroad."~*
Matthew 12:25-30

I was troubled

I believed I was in God's will leaving active military service. But on this new path, I had chosen were lots of bumps, potholes, and speed traps. Some I anticipated! Others were shocking and surprising. In hindsight, I see I stirred up Satan in a big way. He was behind a lot that discouraged me in the years following. My decision led me to dig deep into the written word of God. Such personal study time does not pay financially, so I looked for ways to support myself to augment our family household income. In the job searches that followed, because I was in the Greater Seattle area, I experienced directly the discrimination that existed against military people transitioning into the civilian world. Rejection after rejection! It seemed to me that many of John Kerry's friends and relatives must live in Washington State. I finally took a job I did not really like to put food on the table: selling cars. Seattle was certainly Berkley North in terms of the liberalism I encountered. In this area, conservative values are in the minority. This retired warfighter felt the heat from his honorable service in Vietnam. Like so many others I had heard about since the war ended eight years earlier, I, for the first time, met up with and had to battle a spirit of depression and discouragement. If I had been looking for work in the south or Midwest, where my military service was more appreciated, it would have been a much easier transition. But my dad had recently passed, and my mother was widowed and lived close by in Everett. Also, my father-in-law had died unexpectedly. So, I felt bound to the greater Seattle area. At this time, I was not wearing my past life on my sleeve, but I couldn't lie about what I did in the past either. That anti-war sentiment from the Vietnam War is still strong 45 years later.

All this was developing character and a better understanding of spiritual warfare as I struggled to find my niche as a very new civilian. To write with power and authority, one must have a passion for his subject and experience the battle's ups and downs. The best perspective often comes from an author's personal struggles. Yes, I had experienced fighting overseas, but frankly was a novice in the actual arena I wanted to write about: struggles on the home front how Satan attacks the nation from within. Especially how he uses those you expect would appreciate and want the best for you. Can you identify with King David's experiences chronicled in the Book of Psalms and other books? At the time of my military retirement, I did not know the whole depth of meaning behind the next verse I will quote. To write about spiritual warfare and how to prevail, I had a lot more years and battles to go through before I really understood and could identify with the life of King David, Jesus Christ, and other righteous men and women chronicled in the Bible, what they had to endure and experience such as painful betrayals and rejections.

I started out my political life voting democrat. The first person I voted for was John F Kennedy. He was assassinated. His assassination shocked the nation. It broke many hearts and changed America forever. It was not someone from another nation who plotted this evil betrayal. When the whole story comes out, we will see fellow Americans close to the president behind this terrible deed.

Traitors! I hoped the untold story would come out while President Trump was in authority. If one was prone to depression, the animosity between democrats and republicans could really depress me, for both are in our extended family.

When I was young and naive, I voted democrat. When I wised up, I became a republican. But I now see the corruption on both sides of the political spectrum. I believe most Rino Republicans are concealed democrats. Evil has crossed the aisle in Congress and affects the Republican Party also. I know this. Why? I ran for a state office in Washington State: the House of Representatives. I learned things I did not want to believe possible during that year-long campaign. That was back in 1989. Betray, betrayed, betrayal are nasty words. You find it used only once in the Old Testament: **I Chronicals 12:17** by David. However, you see it often in the Old Testament, for instance: in the life of the warrior, Samson, who Deliah famously betrayed. But God seems to save this word mostly for the New Testament. It is used sixteen times in **the Book of Matthew** alone. Every time Jesus Christ speaking about his coming betrayal by Judas. The scariest verse using this word is found in **Matthew 24:10.**

"...and then shall many be offended and shall betray one another and shall hate one another."

This verse tragically and perfectly describes what we see today in Congress's Halls and across our nation. Traitors are embedded deep into our important institutions across America. The animosity going on right now in politics is really dangerous. We seem almost equally divided along party lines. To win at all costs, many candidates must lie, cheat, and steal. It is so sad to see. Life in politics should show us the best side of the character. But it does not. You can vote for the right candidate and party for the wrong reasons. It is hard to educate ourselves to vote wisely because the press and such tools as google are so one-sidedly partisan. I have mostly focused on the civilian world since I retired from active duty. That was over 37 years ago. That military preoccupation in my young adult life has been let go. I have learned a lot about our supernatural enemy's tactics and strategies against us through civilian eyes since my military retirement. This vantage point has further opened my spiritual eyes and ears. I have read my Bible forwards and backward since this time. I have listened to a lot of teachings from gifted believers. Much of what I have learned has been firsthand through the greatest teacher of all, the Holy Spirit. Many times, I have wished I had never left active duty. Civilian life has not been all sweetness and honey for me. But my decision to leave in 1983 was of the Lord.

I wrote and published a book and then edited it and republished it under another title while speaking around the northwest at every opportunity. For maybe thirteen years, I had a website: **waragoodwarfare.com** until I shut it down in 2018. At this site, I published thirteen other books I had written on the subject of spiritual warfare. Those interested could read and download all for free. This was just one of the growing numbers of internet locations where the truth of the gospel is trumpeted from many different perspectives. And for about eighteen years, I have been the chaplain at the local VFW Post and have published a monthly 400-word column on spiritual warfare for years. In 2018 I thought I was finished writing and talking about war. I prayed about what the Lord wanted me to do next. After a time of waiting, I got one word. MILLENNIALS. That is how the Lord often communicates with me. One word from the Lord is like a sinker on a fishing line for me. Cast it out and see what follows… a string of thoughts and words usually! After the study, I wrote a draft for small towns, an S.O.P., to help struggling millennials. I shared it with one former mayor of a nearby small town. She encouraged me. I have done what I felt led to do. Implementing this program would take money, time, and effort, which I do not have enough of. So, I decided to write one more book to publish.

in the balance

Our nation hangs in the balance in 2020. Many world forces are lining up against us to force us to go in a direction we should not go toward the One World Government! A strong but small minority is trying to lead us back toward our foundings and earlier ideals. I am part of that minority. It seems most Americans are caught up in their own fears and doubts and barely hanging on. Their focus is small, their own survival! Behind all our troubles in this nation is **the Deep State.** The level of pure evil within that dark circle is very seldom recognized. Why? Because they work in darkness and are seldom caught out in the light of day. But just maybe things are turning around for America. Can there be another great awakening? Yes! It is possible. God, against all odds, has given us President Trump to point and lead us in the right direction. And he is a wrecking ball as far as the Deep State is concerned. The more he is attacked, the stronger he becomes. That is a sign he is God's man for the hour.

I wish more Americans were Bible readers. That is a wonderful passion to have. When a change of direction is needed, the Bible is a great place to start looking for answers on how to proceed. Who can you trust? Who are the wolves in sheep's clothing? The word *enemy* is found 382 times in scripture. You find this word just in the **Book of Psalms** 105 times. Behind all personal problems stands a relentless enemy, Satan, and his fallen angels and demon forces. We learn nothing about our true enemies in public schooling or from the mainstream media. That is why most Americans today find themselves in such a quagmire. The Bible is the authority on supernatural power: good and bad. Based on how stuck in the mud many find themselves, it should seem obvious that dark forces using so-called trusted sources are lined up against the righteous. Prayer is our best tactic. Call on the One who saves. But that is the last place most of us turn for help. I love David's cry in **Psalms 3:7**:

"Arise, O LORD; save me, O my God: For thou hast smitten all mine enemies upon the cheek bones; thou hast broken the teeth of the ungodly."
~Psalms 3:7

If you have surrendered your life to Jesus Christ, this is what he says about our enemies. So, even though you can't see God's angels around you and may only be seeing a depressing situation you face at the moment, **Psalms 3:7** is still the truth concerning what you are facing. Faith and trust can carry you through. Do not let fear, doubt, and unbelief rob you of what God is doing that you might not be seeing.

"Lead me, O LORD, in thy righteousness because of mine enemies make thy way straight before my face."~ **Psalms 5:8**

Remember: Life and death are in the power of the tongue. Be careful what you say.

"For David himself said by the Holy Ghost, The LORD said to my Lord, Sit thou on my right hand, till I make thine enemies thy footstool." ~**Mark 12:36**

Believers are sited: *"in heavenly places in Christ Jesus."* Until we are removed from the earth, we do what Jesus did. He proclaimed his Father. We are to proclaim the Name above all names. That name is not found in the Old Testament. It is found 1055 times in the New Testament. There is power in that name when we pray to our Heavenly Father. We have heard the saying: *"With friends like this, who needs enemies."* There is a great separation going on right now. Let the Holy Ghost be your best friend. Whose side are you really on? Many do not want to take sides, but they must. Scripture tells us that the angels will bundle the tares for the fire and those who are saints for salvation. Judgment is coming. We are either on one side or the other. There are areas of our nation that will be judged in a good way and other areas in a terrible way. If you are being moved, pray about it. Maybe you should not resist it. God may be moving you to a safer spot. And for God's sake, don't be ashamed of who you are in Christ.

"For whosoever shall be ashamed of me and of my words, of him shall the Son of man be ashamed when he shall come in his own glory, and in his Father's, and of the holy angels," ~**Luke 2:26**

Suppose you have been betrayed and are hurting; look to God. Repent for personal sins and forgive those who hurt you. The word "betrayal" is found 53 times in the Bible. Except for one verse in **I Chronicals 12:17**, a good story, all the verses in the New Testament concern the betrayal of Jesus Christ. If you have been betrayed, consider it a wound like unto the wounds of Jesus Christ. It is like earning the Medal of Honor in the Lord's army. It is tough to forgive and move beyond unforgiveness, but it is a fight worth waging.

12

CHAIN of COMMAND

The first chain of command we experience is at the family level. The family has been under attack for some time, so who is in authority might not be very apparent. There is a lot of confusion in many families, and it is natural for children to test authority. Right away, many children seem to begin acting like they are in charge. There are many dysfunctional families across our nation! Thank God there are still enough functional families that our nation is not in total free fall from disfunction. Who disciplined you when you needed discipline? In many families, children see a lot of arguing. This is not healthy: certainly not scriptural. Who makes the important decisions? Often there is a division of authority and responsibility. Where does the person at the family level who thinks they are in charge go to for support, advice, and help?

When my dad married my mom: she, my grandmother, and great grandmother, I was told, traveled to China by ship for the marriage ceremony. Dad was a young career Marine officer on a three-year post in China. My future mom arrived in 1938 to a nation at war with Japan. Their ship stopped in Japan for fuel. America had not yet been drawn into the conflict. The European powers England, France, Germany, Italy, and the United States had infantry regiments in Shanghai, protecting their interests. A large international community was located there. Though the Japanese had invaded China, and the war was raging elsewhere in that country, not so in Shanghai. A year later, my mom traveled through two Japanese-occupied zones to get to the Chinese hospital, where a Chinese doctor brought me into the world. In charge of dad's regiment, the Marine Colonel had sent a driver with a military vehicle to drive her to the Chinese hospital where I was born. The first hands to touch me were a Chinese doctor's hands. Dad was on a gunboat 900 miles up the Yangtze River. The Japanese sentries, she told me later when I asked, were very courteous and smiling. *We* all start out as babies, don't we under a different set of circumstances. At his first coming, God also encountered a hostile world as a baby. So meek and innocent! He also, at birth, was under authority:

learned he obedience

*"Who in the days of his flesh, when he had offered up prayers and supplications with strong crying and tears unto him that was able to save him from death, and was heard in that he feared, though he were a Son, yet learned he obedience by the things which he suffered."~ **Hebrews 5: 7-8***

Scripture exhorts that unless we become like babes, we will not enter the kingdom of heaven. Many never reach adulthood. Amazing to me right now is the absence of wisdom and self-discipline surrounding us in the 21st Century. Life is not going well for many at the family level right now. There is a veil of blindness covering many parents.

People are so quick to blame others for problems where they are responsible. The lack of responsibility and accountability in adults is alarming and growing. Look at the millennial generation. The proliferation of narcissists and sociopaths among us is shocking. How can this be? Our parents and grandparents suffered hardship and made sacrifices during the Great Depression, in WWII, and during the Korea War. They, too, made mistakes. But look at the families in trouble now. The seeds of these problems started far earlier. Our nation today is not the one I was raised to believe in. But still an exceptional nation among nations!

are we still exceptional

*"As for my people, children are their oppressors, and women rule over them. O my people, they which lead thee cause thee to err, and destroy the way of thy paths."~ **Isaiah 3:12***

Look around! Some of our leaders act like children when in charge, i.e., Portland, Oregon. Their behavior and decisions often seem childish, rebellious, or irrational. I wonder how some leaders obtained power and why voters would still keep them in authority. Portland, Chicago, and Seattle come to mind. Two thoughts surface here: either they stole votes, or citizens in their communities are unrighteous, naive, and deserve such leaders. God said this is how it would be at the end of days. Godly wisdom is increasingly absent from many decision-making processes across our nation.

*"When the righteous are in authority, the people rejoice: but when the wicked beareth rule the people mourn."~ **Proverbs 29:2***

growing up

What I remember most about my growing up years was the frequent moves and loss of good friends. It seems I was starting from scratch about the time I was figuring things out: having to make new neighborhood friends, first day in a new school, everyone a stranger! Having to win over new teachers and classmates! When you are new, it is usually harder. Peer circles are already established. I was a military brat growing up. A part of a military household! WWII was followed quickly by the Korean War. The Cold War loomed big during my growing years.

Days from my first birthday, dad's three years in China were over. He was ordered back to the states. Maybe a year later, the Marine Regiment in China was withdrawn to the Philippines, Pearl Harbor was attacked, and the war began. Those Marines my dad served with in China and a greater force of army soldiers: 450,000 men, were cut off and were forced to surrender to the Japanese in the Phillippines. General MacArthur fled by submarine. A dismal start to the Second World War. The movie, MIDWAY, shows how precarious things really were at that time. That DVD shows a little of what was going on in the Pacific. My dad spent his first nine months in Guadacanal at that time. Also, there were the Atlantic and European theaters of war.

The 18,000 officers and Marines suddenly were intensely involved in preparations to fight the Japanese nation. America was soon in a fight for its survival on two fronts: the Atlantic and Pacific. By the end of the fighting three and a half years later, those 18,000 marines had expanded to 450,000 warfighters, just in the Marine Corps. And in our current day, you need to join the increasingly desperate spiritual warfare fight.

My dad was called home for a few months of career schooling early on. I got a brief taste of kindergarten schooling, maybe three weeks. Then he was ordered back overseas. We went to mom's folk's home in Everett, Washington, to await his return. Not counting his three years in China and nine months in Iceland after the Japanese attack, he spent five years during the two wars overseas as a warfighter. He would soon be a two-war Marine. I do not remember much about that period of time except things like falling into a poison ivy patch and developing a terrible itch, and what the outside of our two-story brick apartment complex looked like in Quantico, Virginia. I was five.

First grade was my first real experience away from my mother. I nowexperienced another authority outside the family chain of command! Dad was often gone from home for my first eleven years. He was ordered back into China after the war ended with Japan for eleven months to supervise the Japanese's surrender to the Chinese who hated the Japanese. His battalion helped prevent the wholesale slaughter of the Japanese in China. My mother was my only real stability during those early years. But behind her was a loving husband and provider. But she was who I looked to in the family chain of command. I knew dad mostly from a picture on the coffee table during my early years. We all need at least one other faithful adult to depend on in such times. I appreciate and always will those who bear the burden of command, which requires uncommon family sacrifice. It was about the survival of our nation during those years.

I vaguely remember times of crying and fearfulness. I sometimes heard mom quietly crying alone while dad was gone. Looking back now from my own experience, I see it was a very lonely time for mom. That first year in first grade, I caught everything that was going around among my classmates: Mumps! Measles! Chicken box, flu-colds. I remember lots of headaches and stuffiness! This all led up to my first and only surgical operation. Tonsils and adenoids had to come out. After that, I was able to breathe through my nose comfortably for the first time.

a chain of command beyond the family

Missing a lot of schooling caused me to repeat first grade. Not a great start to my K-16 learning experience. I was setting the example for two younger brothers. In later years the added body weight, height, and age turned this early emotional setback into a real advantage in high school sports (football, basketball, and track.) The added weight and height helped. I went through four years of high school with three major moves to three different states: Virginia, Pennsylvania, and South Carolina. I joined every sports team I could to more quickly make friends the best I could each year.

What does this have to do with the chain of command? Dad, Mom, teachers, coaches are our authority figures in our early years. They wield power. I experienced these early chains of command, where people were in authority over me. I learned who I could trust. Some are not so fortunate to experience the love I did. I was told I was an easy child to raise. I wanted to please. We see some rebel against the systems they are raised in for differing and often authentic reasons. Someone wrote a book: All I Really Need to Know I learned in Kindergarten.

For me, my early years were such a blur with frequent moves. Like a Marine in boot camp, I learned early I was under authority and needed their approval to be the best I could be. As an adult, I experienced boot camp.

In military boot camps, one of the great lessons taught is about the importance of the chain of authority and what it means. I learned this lesson well. I did have to learn new names and faces much more often than most. I think a better understanding of identity, who you are, can come with such frequent moves and certainly during boot camp. It did for me. When I was finally done with schooling, I was ready to step into adult living. Or so I thought.

the need for transformation

Like kindergarten, where we are supposed to learn everything that matters in life, boot camp seemed to expose me to what mattered as a warfighter. Almost a DNA. change is required to graduate! In many ways, one becomes a different person. We feel much the same, but our survival skills are certainly given a kick start. The impact can be life-changing. And it is capped off with a parade field graduation ceremony that is awesome. A defining moment in life for sure. Except for those who fail to graduate! That would be terrible, I expect. Advancing through civilian classroom schooling, I got a taste and sense of authority, responsibility, accountability, integrity, and such. But it was not to be compared with what a hard-nosed drill instructor can teach.

A lot of head knowledge is acquired in K through university! Some of it useful for sure. But does public schooling really prepare most for life beyond the home? I don't think so. I wonder if that is what the 40 percent of millennials who are giving their age group such a bad name at the moment really need? Right now, it seems they need a boot camp experience to snap them out of their funk. Maybe that would transform them.

When a man goes through boot camp and other such intense training experiences leading up to the stress and terrors of actual combat, he truly comes away with an understanding of authority, power, and the importance of the chain of command. This is seldom learned academically. A heart change is needed. Radical transformations do happen in homes and in civilian schooling to get us beyond our terrible twos. But if that does not happen, maybe a national boot camp experience is in order. Several things happen to transform us from civilians to soldiers in all military boot camps: no matter which uniformed service operates the boot camp! And yes, future officers go through boot camp, too; it's just called officer candidate training. I can assure you it is just as intense, maybe more so. The importance of the chain of command is ironed into one's memory bank. Insubordination is not tolerated. If one did not learn the importance of memorizing in his civilian schooling days, he certainly will in boot camp. Not doing so triggers unpleasant consequences such as extra pushups and other forms of deprivation. Most come away from such experiences transformed. Your awareness of what surrounds you gets better. Blindness in

179

combat can be fatal. You learn that life is not always nice. It can be a hostile place. You learn vigilance and skills to fight back, to survive.

Boot camp is a necessary evil to transform a person quickly into a man he might not become otherwise. At least not quickly. Civilians do not survive in combat. Soldiers have a chance to survive and prosper. It takes a boot camp experience to effect the needed change. We need more than schooling to change our knowledge and thinking. Training affects the mind, will, and emotions, and certainly the body physically. It separates you from friends and family actually in a healthy way. You grow up quickly. You are alone in a semi-hostile environment for nine to thirteen weeks. If you cannot or will not adapt, you fail and are rejected. But to fail is not made easy, for there is no easy escape from boot camp rigors. You experience a definite chain of command in boot camp few experience at the family level. The drill instructor is a highly competent teacher, unlike many parents. The one in charge just above you, the drill instructor, seems hell-bent on making your life miserable. Nothing you do is right in his eyes at first.

"But if ye be without chastisement, whereof all are partakers, then are ye bastards and not sons." ~**Hebrews 12:8**

Yes, there can be chastisement at the family level and in the public school system, but not like in military boot camps. You learn quickly to please your superiors. Above "the man" is an officer whom you do not see often but plans and supervises every aspect of your experience, which has been designed to quickly change you into someone who knows how to fight and follow orders. Those up the line of authority have even more authority and power than your drill sergeant. There are the captains, majors, colonels, and generals above your everyday experiences supporting you in indirect ways.

The actual pictures of those above you in the chain of command all the way up to the President of the United States are posted on the walls of your barracks and in the classrooms. This chain of command is drilled into your mind. You memorize all their names and faces. It becomes an important reality. Unlike the spiritual reality that most have only a vague understanding of.

At every command level are chaplains. They will teach you about the supernatural chain of command at the top of the military chain of command if you ask. In many families and in today's public-school systems, this spiritual authority is not taught at all. Most graduate and head into adulthood with no understanding at all of the supernatural or political realms and how they influence their lives. They have been essentially blinded though they think they can see and hear.

In boot camp, you learn about the power and authority that surround you. And about following orders quickly and efficiently. You learn how to work as part of a team—not adapting instantly to personal orders triggers pushups, sit-ups, pullups, and other forms of punishments until your muscles scream for relief! You toughen up. You get smarter. Yes, in civilian schooling and life, you do experience authority but not like in the military world.

real authority

Boot camp and the chain of command is all about authority. To graduate from boot camp is, for some, the proudest day of their life. It is a big deal. Some do not measure up and are discharged. They would not emotionally or physically survive possible coming trials, putting others at risk. In war, even some declared fit don't survive. The man who made your life miserable, the drill instructor, quickly you learn, is the most important man in your life. Slowly you learn to appreciate him. At graduation, you proudly introduce him to any family members who come to your graduation; for some, no family members show up. The recruit platoon is your new family; friends made at camp fill in emotional gaps from poor parenting. Many become very close during their shared afflictions. A family forged under the intense pressure that comes from all directions! Fellow Marine graduates that you are proud to call brothers. Other than actual combat, there is hardly an experience I can name that forges such brotherhood as the boot camp experience. Many are woven so tightly together that 30 or 40 years later, they look forward to meeting again at a camp reunion. More important for many than any high school reunion!

A man may not remember most of his primary and secondary school teachers in later life. But his boot camp drill instructor he never forgets! His high school principal might not remember his name or face, but the captain who led his boot camp company will remember men who stood out.

That dislike he initially had for his tormentors slowly turns into grudging respect and then into great admiration as he sees the astonishment on his family and friend's faces back home. What boot camp can do is remarkable. Healthy transformations are essential to success in life.

Saluting, troop formations, marches, and the endless hours of all kinds of drills, classroom time, and intense physical exercise hardwire what is being taught into one's being. Seldom does civilian academic education lead to such a transformation. And for some comes actual combat and the life and death decisions that result from time spent in such a crucible. A time of great testing! Succeed or fail and its lifelong consequences!

As a lieutenant in charge of a Marine platoon or a captain in charge of a rifle company in combat, I made decisions that had life and death impacts on men's lives. It is a terrible responsibility, wielding such power. At such times men must be under competent leadership following orders from a legitimate authority. As important as this all is, it pales in significance to the importance of understanding your spiritual chain of command. All real power comes from above, especially earthly power. Few civilians ever learn this. More alarming still, many veterans never translate this understanding into being able to fight the good fight spiritually after they leave active duty. Too few ever really look to God for the help they need and will find from God. Such a shame! So, why is understanding the chain of commands you operate under in life so important? Because no one can always go it alone. You are always under authority, whether you realize it or not. We have a level of support many do not understand or know how to appropriate. They are just out there doing their thing and often winging it! But if we are acting within the law, we have a legal right to do what we do even when we feel we are all alone. It is when one gets out from under lawful authority that things begin to go wrong. We lose our legal covering. The book of **Numbers**, chapter 30, is about vowing a vow, and it is being tied to authority at the family level. A very important chapter you have probably never heard preached or taught. Study it! Very valuable insight!

In closing, I will say your chain of command is your official support system. All organizations have them. If you are not properly listened to, you can appeal. And there are spiritual entities that affect decision-making. It is always wise to pray. Prayer affects all outcomes. Look at Mathew 16.19; you have the power in Christ to "bind" and "loose." Study these words in your bible. You are not alone as a believer.

But about bad leadership, what did Jesus say to his disciples after his encounter with such leaders?

Let them alone: they be blind leaders of the blind. And if the blind lead the blind, both shall fall into the ditch."
~Matthew 15:14

13

TACTICS AND STRATEGY

For 25 years of my life, I was a student of physical warfare. Other than family and sports, my primary interests were subjects like leadership and this chapter's focus. I have been officially retired from being called back to active service since 1992. There has not been a real reason to maintain my proficiency in the natural realm of military skills for almost 30 years. Anything I had to contribute on this front became obsolete long ago, one would think. But if that were true, why do older military scholars teach midshipmen and cadets at our military academies about ancient battles and the thinking, actions, successes, and failures of long-gone warfighters who died centuries ago? Solomon said it: *"There is nothing new under the sun."* Tactics and strategic thinking never really age. Yes, weapons, means of transportation, technology, and communications are always advancing, not so with the eleven principles of warfare. They are timeless. They can be applied to all wars: political, economic, social, or physical, no matter the age one lived in.

a story

Long ago, my rifle company was ordered to cross South Vietnam's border into Laos, an adjacent nation, to conduct a night raid and be back across the border by dawn. My regimental commander, Colonel Robert Barrow, a future 4-star general and commandant, had an overall strategy he was executing. Once inside Laos, I choose a particular tactic to disrupt best whatever military opportunity I encountered. I choose the ambush tactic because of the possibility of significant enemy movement on an important road network through the Ashau Valley that night. If you desire to get an overview of the operation from the Colonel's point of view, read about Operation Dewey Canyon. (the last great operation for the Marines in Vietnam before they were withdrawn) It is on the internet posted by Wikipedia! I have already written in detail about this rifle company ambush for the Marine Corps Gazette Magazine published in January 1984 titled Night Ambush. It can be found on the internet by anyone. I also published that story in a book I later wrote, FORWARD MARCH. Later I republished it after adding some new material. It was titled SECRET WEAPON: MEN OVERCOMING CHAOS. Both available for purchase as used books. Additionally, I maintained a website for years (www.waragoodwarfare.com), which I reactivated on January 1, 2021, where anyone can read for free what I had written, including ten others never published books. Everything I write is from a Christian believer's perspective.

I would like to briefly say something about the rifle company action that forced the withdrawal of the enemy artillery 122 mm howitzer battery that we ambushed. It was engaging our regiment and had fired over ten thousand rounds at the regiment. They were moving away from the infantry assault on their firing position by A 1/9 to a safer position where they could resume their firing on our regimental advance in and around the border with Laos.

Lieutenant Wesley Fox, commanding Alpha Company 1st battalion 9th Marines, won the Medal of Honor for his heroism, as did a platoon commander. He later advanced to the rank of full colonel of Marines. My son, Steve, met him when he was going through officer candidate school to become a Marine officer. Wesley was the Commanding Officer of the officer candidate program at that time. I had given my son a copy of a book I never published, which was an amalgamation of much of my thinking and observations at that time. If you run across one of my friends still on active duty, I told him to give it to him. I had a premonition he would meet someone. I did not know Colonel Fox was at Quantico, but God knew.

He was standing at an inspection at attention, and Colonel Fox stepped before him and spoke. "You must be Dave Winecoff's son. You look just like him when he was your age. How is he? Steve answered. Fine, Sir. He gave me a book to give to you. He received an invitation to visit his quarters the next weekend for dinner and to bring the book. Steve met his wife, whom I had never met. We were mainly wartime friends. We had not been stationed together following the war. Talk about speaking of a small world!

Many people try to engineer such meetings to incur worldly favor using worldly tactics and strategies. The Lord of Heaven and Earth does not work that way. He causes what the church sometimes refers to as divine encounters or appointments. My son's meeting up with this acquaintance from my past was one of those times. It put a draft of a yet-to-be-published book in his hands after I had retired from the Corps. At that time, I was struggling to make my way in the civilian world as a writer. His counsel to my son? Get your dad to publish this book! There is a lot of wisdom in it. Every Marine should read it. At that time, I was under a lot of attacks. Eventually, it did get posted on my website for free. It was free to anyone who was doing any kind of search on subjects I was interested in. I never made a dime off those writings. It was all for the Lord at a time I was struggling financially. For sixteen years between my two marriages, I battled my demons of loneliness and rejection after a failed 26-year marriage.

my father's mother

Her name was NeNe; my grandmother lived her whole life in Atlanta, Georgia. I never really got to know her one-on-one as I never lived in Atlanta, and only briefly for a year lived in Fort Benning, Georgia, two hours away. My military schooling kept me quite busy. So except for a few brief visits growing up while I was still in my parent's home and a few times coming through on the way to somewhere else, I never really got to know my dad's side of the family.

But I know this. I have lived a better life than many and probably most. She was a woman of prayer. She was a lifelong Roman Catholic. Every morning of her adult life, she went to morning mass at 0630, rain or shine. She lived four blocks from the church and always walked to and from. I do not know if it is true, but I have heard with daily mass attendance, one cycles through the entire Bible in three years.

She was a woman of prayer, and her eldest son, my dad, was a career Marine officer in the thick of things during WWII and Korea. An uncle and great uncle were marine officers, also. Neither dad nor I ever earned a purple heart by sustaining a combat wound. Go figure! Prayer makes a difference. It matters not the particular way of faith you were born into. The Christian who prays to the Father in heaven in the precious Name of Jesus has an impact we will never really know about this side of heaven.

divine encounters

In the book of Acts, we find the word encounter only one place in scripture, a marvelous book for a believer to pour-over. It can open up a deep understanding of the supernatural realm and the Helper God has sent into the world. The Holy Ghost wants to work through us if only we will invite him in and let him operate through us! With the Holy Ghost in our life, there is no need for formal education in tactics and strategy because the LORD of heaven and earth already has Satan figured out and knows how to block his every attempt to kill, capture and destroy.

*"Then certain philosophers of the Epicureans, and of the Stoics, <u>encountered</u> him. And some said, What will this babbler say? Others said, He seemeth to be a setter forth of strange gods: because he preached unto them Jesus and the resurrection."~ **Acts 17:18***

Paul was bold in the Lord. He had had a life-changing encounter with Jesus Christ on the road to Damascus to kill Christians. There was murder in his heart before his transformation. After his full surrender to the Lord, the tables began to turn for him. The zealots were now out to kill him.

bold direction

It is clear soldiers need prayers and backing from those back home. If nothing else, the Vietnam War proved that. It is a wonder more highly decorated military men don't speak out publicly and forcefully about this need. They must know unless spiritually blinded by sin. of the impact of prayers on their personal lives! Why is it so hard for public men to talk publicly about spiritual matters? Because the god haters do not make it easy on them if they do. There is a cost for those who do speak out. God bless those who do.

We see President Lincoln did so during the terrible American civil war when Americans fought against fellow Americans in a bloody civil war. That national wound has still not healed—over a 600,000 dead over whether or not to set the slaves free. Mostly white men died! Satan is adept at keeping past hatreds festering. The division over slavery and states' rights went right down to the family level. Brother against brother! One could effectively make the case that division won't heal until Christ returns to bring peace to this troubled nation and earth. General Lee surrendered to General Grant way back in 1865, 150 some years ago. His statute I read was just taken down due to the BLM protests. Generals and admirals are concerned about the unity of command for a reason. It is a vital principle of warfare.

Religion is a very controversial subject, as are politics and sex. It is worldly wisdom for leaders to avoid such controversies. Most keep such opinions they have to themselves while on active duty. Really, the parents, pastors, priests, and rabbis have the greater duty to remind people publicly of the importance of prayers and godly living. One of the great untold secrets of all time is that God does take sides. He will help those who love him no matter the side of the argument or dispute they find themselves on. He has already helped by giving those who believe in Him supernatural tools to affect all outcomes. These tools are laid out in writings in the Bible. Why so many are ignorant of these tools should not be a mystery. Satan is a master at hiding important discoveries in plain sight.

the right direction

Strategy has to do with a plan for winning. Jesus Christ stands outside our realities, waiting to be invited into our situations and lives. (**Revelation 3:20**) Our Heavenly Father has sent the Holy Spirit as a guide and helper, but so many put him on the shelf. The Bible speaks clearly about this. In so many lives and organizations, it is all about what is popular and trendy rather than obedience to the Word of God. God does not look at success and failure the way we do. The Holy Bible shows us God's will. We are wise to go against what seems popular in the world. Many pick and choose what they want to believe, skipping over difficult passages in the Bible. God has laid out a timeline over which his plan is playing out. Prophecies show us what will happen in the future despite what man desires. He knows the end from the beginning. Many prophecies have already come to pass exactly as he warned us would happen. That is how he authenticates his word. That he can be trusted! The Bible could not have been written by men.

The problem is most of the world does not listen to him or heed his warnings. Most have a different worldview than Christians. It should bother us when we see a brother or sister going along with worldly trends and at odds with what the Bible has to say. Christianity is being torn apart. Just look at the division. Can we trust the Bible when most people are just going along with the spirit of the age we live in? Who can we trust if not the Holy Spirit inside us?

A major problem in many churches is that so many who confess Christ do not read and study all the Bible. They have no real way of judging what is being taught from their pulpit on Sunday mornings or what is being ignored. It can all sound so good and inspiring. But is what we are hearing that is popular really taking us off track? When we go back into the world on Monday morning, will those who listen to our words and watch our actions see any difference in us that will inspire them to seek out Jesus Christ on their own? Can the Christian God be trusted and depended upon when they see that a follower of Christ lacks integrity in the marketplace? Satan uses academic scholars to discredit the Bible also. Christian truth is under attack from within and without. God clearly can be trusted. But so few are knowledgeable enough about spiritual matters even to know and teach the promises he has made in his written word for those who confess they follow him.

"Put not your trust in princes, nor in the son of man in whom there is no help." ~Psalm 146:3

Does this verse mean trust, but verify? When we trust other humans, do we do so carefully and wisely? Don't be beguiled by smooth speech, impressive titles, and resumes into actions that run counter to the written word of God. We

191

all need a plume line to measure our actions and those of others. We must choose wisely where our standards come from. What is this standard if not the written word of God?

above the struggle

God himself is above the struggle in our world. The Son of God came into the world for the particular purpose of salvation, redemption, to set an example, and to destroy the works of the devil. It should be clear he desires to indwell his fully surrendered saints. The Creator of all is above the fray. He is pure Spirit. Not so Satan, his fallen angels, and the demons. They are spirits and have everything to lose in the end. For they too are created beings! They think in terms of winning and losing. And are increasingly in a rage because they know they have already lost the fight, and the end is drawing near. They have a strategy and employ tactics against us who believe, love God, and serve him in this world. We are their principal targets. They are clearly our enemies. We need to understand who they are and what they are trying to accomplish. The Bible tells us a lot about them. Even better, it informs us of the help that God offers us and has already provided us so we can prevail in this fallen world. We are in a struggle to the death or our rapture. We clearly must keep the end in view laid out in **the Book of Revelation,** or we will lose our way or never find it in the first place:

"And the devil that deceived them was cast into the lake of fire and brimstone where the beast and the false prophet are and shall be tormented day and night for ever and ever." ~ Revelation 20:10

Revelation tells us about the final judgments of God that are coming soon. The last five verses of chapter 20 are very sobering. I have not heard a sermon preached from this text in a local church, which is too bad.

Too many of us have a distorted, unrealistic view of the afterlife.

"And the devil that deceived them was cast into the lake of fire and brimstone, where the beast and the false prophet are, and shall be tormented day and night for ever and ever. And I saw a great white throne, and him that sat on it, from whose face the earth and the heaven fled away; and there was found no place for them. And I saw the dead, small and great, stand before God; and the books were opened: and another book was opened, which is the book of life: and the dead were judged out of those things which were written in the books, according to their works. And the sea gave up the dead which were in it; and death and hell delivered up the dead which were in them: and they were judged every man according to their works. And death and hell were cast into the lake of fire. This is the second death. And whosoever was not found written in the book of life was cast into the lake of fire." **~Revelation 20: 10-15**

sober-minded

If the above passage does not wake people up who are asleep spiritually, I fear for them. Most millennials are likely never to hear this preached. When I shut down my spiritual warfare website (which is now back up), the Lord gave me one word. "Millennials!" I do not think just the family can help the average unsuccessful millennial. I worry about their spiritual condition. Most are not in a church. Many show no real interest in spiritual matters. Only God can help them, and many are not looking in his direction.

"Young men likewise exhort to be sober minded, In all things showing thyself a pattern of good works: in doctrine showing uncorruptness, gravity, sincerity, Sound speech that cannot be condemned; that he that is of the contrary part may be ashamed, having no evil thing to say of you." **~Revelation 20:11-15**

*"Wherefore gird up the loins of your mind, be sober and hope to the end for the grace that is to be brought unto you at the revelation of Jesus Christ;"~ **I Peter 1:13***

This is sound advice for us all, but particularly for those who have no clue to the real reality. Life is so much beyond what one sees and hears that affects us in the natural realm. The spiritual realm is so much more realistic. If only we could see with spiritual eyes and hear with spiritual ears.

We all want to go to heaven. But hell is our destiny if we have no one praying for us and never accept Jesus Christ.

finding the way

I do not think we have to be all that smart in the eyes of this world. God seems to sort things out no matter the particular talents or lack thereof we are born with. He is the great evener outer. He keeps an account and has lots of angels to help, watch, and record. We see the Book of Life mentioned nine times! **Philippians 4:3** and elsewhere **in the book of Revelation.**

"He that overrcometh, the same shall be clothed in white raiment; and I will not blot out his name out of the book of life, but I will confess his name before my Father, and before his angels."
~**Revelation 3:5**

So, what is the winning strategy? To throw one's self on the mercy of God! To repent often and forgive always! To work hard, not to be prideful! And to show mercy whenever possible! And when attacked verbally to turn the other cheek! Yes, we must fight against evil. But the most effective way is in prayer in secret.

How much time in the course of the day should we be praying? My two grandmothers, who are both gone now, both had quiet, gentile spirits. Both were good examples in my family. I am so grateful for their love and support. I expect to see them both in eternity. They will be called blessed by those of us who reach heaven partly due to their prayers. Certainly not because of our own efforts. Finding that path leading to the saving knowledge of Jesus Christ is difficult. But He is the only way.

lies and accusations

Many make their living using tactics such as lies, blaming, and accusations. They keep the flames of division alive, greatly weakening their opponents and our nation. Who would do that? Unfortunately, many do it knowingly, some just unwittingly. There are devoted communist insiders who are undercover. They are working for those who hate us in other nations. Why? To achieve their Machiavellian goals of changing the direction of history to a one-world government.

In college, I learned leadership tools like Management by Objectives. The importance of setting long-term goals. Short-term goals, etc. Techniques to get the team effectively moving in the smart direction. Such techniques are viewed as critical in achieving victory. They certainly proved their worth in World War II. These strategies and objectives were greatly responsible for the rapidly expanding business explosion in the aftermath of that great war. It contributed to making us the greatest world superpower of our time. American industry and power are now everywhere around the globe. As great as setting goals may be, it pales in comparison to falling in line with the plans of the living God. His tactics will always trump those of the enemy of our souls.

The Bible describes the times we are in with the phrase: *"wars and rumors of wars."* There are many books, articles, and publications for sale, discussing winning and losing strategies; how to succeed using tactics in actual warfare and in economic competition. Many organizations have them written into their governing manuals. Churches discuss this subject in terms of how to grow their organizations. There are only a few pastors who discuss spiritual warfare from their pulpits. A few more might tackle this topic in a small group bible study. But for the most part, believers are quite ignorant of such matters.

I tell you from personal experience it is hard to find a local church where the pastor is trying to put the supernatural tools God has given us all into the hand of household leaders: Fathers and mothers, husbands, and wives! I saw one recent study where the teacher said in his research, only two percent of the sermons in one study found that spiritual warfare is being addressed from the pulpit.

A few years ago, I made a couple of appointments with a church pastor where we had been in church for close to a year to discuss the direction he was taking his church. My wife and I didn't like that when he was absent on a Sunday, he had a single, unmarried woman, a close friend of his wife, and not even a member, filling in for him. It was at odds with Paul's advice concerning placing women over men. He was not open to scriptural advice. So, we left that church. We have not shared with friends the particular reason we left. He had competent men there to fill in for him. He was a young, smart modernist following the present cultural trend of choosing a woman for leadership when good family men are available. He does not have an elder board advising him. It is his first parish after gaining leadership experience in several college parachurch organizations. He has an engaging personality and is well-liked.

in the final analysis

I want to close this chapter by talking about our personal habits and the regrets we all have. The Bible tells us that deep calls unto deep.

"Deep calleth unto deep at the noise of thy waterspouts: all thy waves and thy billows are gone over me." ~ **Psalm 42: 7**

The Lord in many places is called "deep," and did you know you were made in his image. So somewhere in you is "deep" that another human being cannot touch. Only God can reach that place inside you that needs to be touched for you to fully come alive.

Last night, my wife talked about her children's needs, who are struggling and need to be addressed. She had a download concerning the following scripture.

"Because strait is the gate, and narrow is the way, which leadeth unto life, and few there be that find it."~ **Matthew 7:14**

We all want to help our children and ourselves. Certain personal habits can be killers. Often, they come about because of regrets. A love that was denied us or one that turned sour, etc. When we just cannot seem to get past a great disappointment, it is easy to blame another or that situation or God. As we look around, we see others that are stuck in time; it seems. They cannot get by a past disappointment or regret. How to help them? How to help ourselves? A bad habit develops and begins to take us over and out.

God has sent us help to fix in us and others what needs fixing. He is the Holy Ghost. All we have to do is invite him into our lives, but many believers never do, and it is so sad. The path is very narrow that takes us to heaven, and few find that path, and others cannot seem to stay on it. How do we get past our regrets and shortcomings? The bad habits in our lives!

That is why a loving Father sent the Holy Spirit to this earth. To help us! Will you let him fix what needs fixing? Most never do! With him helping you, who needs to worry about tactics or strategy? What we choose to believe determines how much truth we can receive.

14

DECISIONS

*"Multitudes, multitudes in the valley of <u>decision</u>: for the day of the LORD is near in the valley of <u>decision</u>."~ **Joel 3:14***

This quote is the only time God uses this English word in the KJV Bible. It is such an important word. The word rings with decisiveness, the opposite of doublemindedness. It signifies a change in direction. The particular verse above refers to a planned judgment day in the future. That coming day of darkness and gloom is more likely in this decade than ever before in history. I am 82 years of age and in excellent health. If that day does not playout soon, I will be greatly surprised. But in a small way, it plays out for each and every one of us in our own lives. We all have an appointed time to die. Will we accept Christ as our Lord and Savior before that appointed day? God knows the end from the beginning. He knows the pivotal point beyond which we have no more time left. We will have used up our last opportunity. This thought is sobering. At some point in time, if we keep putting off such an important decision, we lose the opportunity. In that valley on that particular day referenced above is such a time: it is known as the Day of the LORD.

the course of a life

When I look back throughout my life, I see I have been blessed despite some bad decisions. There are others who might not come to this conclusion when looking back over their lives. They may see more troubles than blessings. But not so with me. We all have bad things happen to us that seemed out of our control. Some that still affect us decades later! Why?

Because we are human, we are mistake-prone despite our best intentions. All decisions do have consequences.

I once asked my dad in his later years if he would change anything if he were to go back in time. *"Not a thing!"* he said. He responded with no pause to reflect. At the time, I couldn't understand his thinking. When I asked him that question at that particular time, I had one specific thing on my mind I would have liked to have changed. Now for my life, I cannot remember what was weighing heavy on me at that particular time. God works everything for good. I see it now. Much more clearly than when I asked dad that question!

"The steps of a good man are ordered by the LORD: and he delighteth in his way." ~Psalms 37:23

stepping out

In 1983 I decided to retire from active service to get involved in the unseen war raging across our nation. Within a decade, my son, Steve, decided to become a Marine officer. While he was stationed at Camp Lejeune, North Carolina, I got a call from him that he was involved in what I probably saw in the news. He was deploying. That evening I saw on national TV the President of Haiti threatening us. He said: *"You have the Marines, but we have Voodo, and we will be victorious."* I sat down and wrote a lengthy letter based on the curses that came against us in Vietnam and the damages Asian witchcraft caused in the aftermath of that tragic war; what I learned about spiritual warfare and its effects on veterans were mailed, two copies express to him that day. His wife rushed down to the ship, which was about to sail, and it was delivered to him. He gave both copies to the two assigned chaplains he knew. Later he told me, as they sailed around Haiti waiting to go ashore, the chaplains read contents of the letter over the public address system during their evening talks over the ship's communications systems.

What happened? After secret negotiations, the Marines went ashore peacefully. They were there for one month. There was one squad-level firefight, one ammo dump exploded from an incoming mortar round, and one helicopter crashed. I read all this in the newspapers. The Marines experienced no casualties except for one sprained ankle. When the Marines were replaced by an army division: within the first week, there was a soldier who committed suicide. Prayer based on spiritual intelligence gets results. To this very day, Haiti experiences many problems because many there reject Jesus Christ and because they embrace witchcraft.

leaders and followers

We all know leaders make organizational decisions affecting others. They will be judged for the quality of those decisions. And what about those who are their followers who carry out their decisions, good and bad? We are all decision-makers and followers. The Bible has much to say using these two words in the subtitle above. The word lead or led is used 22 times.

"Lead me, O LORD, in thy righteousness because of mine enemies; make thy way straight before my face."
~Psalms 5: 8

What a wonderful personal declaration this is. Just typing out this verse encouraged me to declare this over my life today. How about you? I would like to share four verses: Psalms 27: 11, 61: 2, 68: 18, and 125: 5. But for the sake of brevity, we will move on to the book of **Proverbs**:

"When thou goest, it shall <u>lead</u> thee; when thou sleepest, it shall keep thee; and when thou awakest, it shall talk with thee" ~Proverbs 6: 22

"I <u>lead</u> in the way of righteousness, in the midst of the paths of judgment." ~Proverbs 8: 20

And look at these two verses in the book of **Matthew**:

"Then was Jesus <u>led</u> up of the Spirit into the wilderness to be tempted of the devil."
~Matthew 4: 1

"And <u>lead</u> us not into temptation but deliver us from evil: For thine is the kingdom, and the power, and the glory, forever. Amen."~ Matthew 6: 13

Do you see the value of taking time to reflect on the power of words in such scriptures? I pray you do.

Let's finish looking at the word lead or led with verses from three more books:

"For as many as are <u>led</u> by the Spirit of God, they are the sons of God." ~Romans 8: 14

The above verse motivates me to want to be known publicly as a follower of Jesus Christ and a Holy Ghost man. To be also seen by our Heavenly Father as a son of God.

"But if ye be <u>led</u> of the Spirit, ye are not under the law." ~**Galatians 5: 18**

Another vital reason to be led by the Spirit is you won't be led by the world, the flesh, or the devil.

"For of this sort are they which creep into houses, and <u>lead</u> captive silly women laden with sins, <u>led</u> away with divers lusts, Ever learning, and never able to come to the knowledge of the truth."
~**II Timothy 3: 6-7**

Does this passage cause you to think of any particular women in leadership right now? Who do you wonder about concerning their hidden intentions? There is much written about good and bad examples of leadership to be found in the Bible. If you do not learn how to discern between good and bad leadership, you can never be used much by God to influence others. The phrase *"<u>Because he wholly followed</u>"* is found several times early in the Bible. What we always see following is a blessing. Just one example:

" And Moses swore on that day, saying, Surely the land whereon thy feet have trodden shall be thine inheritance, and thy children's forever, <u>because thou hast wholly followed the LORD</u> my God."
~**Joshua 14: 9-10**

Here are a couple more verses well worth studying out. **Judges 2:12, Proverbs 15: 9, and Isaiah 5:11.** Also, in **Matthew,** there are 27 verses worth looking at. Here is just one example:

"And he saith unto them, <u>follow</u> me, and I will make you fishers of men." **Matthew 4: 19**

We often read Jesus saying: *"Follow me"* in the gospel writings. And just as often the phrase: *"And the crowd followed him,"*

*"And when he was entered into a ship, his disciples followed him." **Matthew 8: 23***

Study also **9: 27, 10: 38, 12: 15, 16: 24, 19: 2, 19: 28, 20: 34, and 26: 38 in Matthew**. These verses are repeated because of their importance in **Mark, Luke, and John's** accounts of Jesus' public ministry.

Following these two words through the Bible is worth a college degree in leadership studies. It is well worth our time to study and meditate on the use of these two words in the Bible!

hardening your heart

Twice in the book of **Hebrews,** we are warned not to harden our hearts to the voice of God. Why? For destruction can come suddenly! In chapter three, we see how Israel provoked God 40 years in the desert after their supernatural exodus from Egypt.

*"While it is said, today if ye will hear his voice harden not your hearts as in the provocation." **Hebrews 3:5***

There are many warnings in scripture given to those acting foolishly. It is folly to provoke the living God. Here is a warning in chapter three.

*"While it is said, today if ye will hear his voice, harden not your hearts, as in the provocation. For some, when they had heard, did provoke howbeit not all that came out of Egypt by Moses. But with whom was he grieved forty years? Was it not with them that had sinned, whose carcasses fell in the wilderness? And to whom swore he that they should not enter into his rest, but to them that believed not? So, we see that they could not enter in because of unbelief. Let us, therefore, fear, lest a promise being left us of entering into his rest, any of you should seem to come short of it." ~**Hebrews 3:15-4:1***

Unbelief is a grievous sin. Those who never study the word of God don't even know when they are in unbelief. The Hebrew slaves God freed from Egypt made personal decisions to choose unbelief that resulted in all but two of that generation perishing in the desert over the next 40 years. Not one of those who crossed the Red Sea who were over twenty years of age made it except Joshua and Caleb. They both entered the promised land because of their faith. Those who ignore many passages of scripture and pick and choose what to believe will find it will not go well for them either. Decisions and actions made that ignore the wisdom found in the Bible turn out badly for such people. They produce consequences that cause eventual hardships. We should all undertake not to make major decisions that cause debt. We should look to those who love us and know us intimately before making important life decisions. I have made choices that did not seem unreasonable to me that later impacted my life in ways that were totally unexpected and not good. Looking back, I see how I acted independently and did not seek council first. Never a wise action! When it comes to any and all-important decisions, we should bathe them in prayer.

"The **steps** *of a good man are* **ordered** *by the* **Lord***: and he delighteth in his way."*
~**Psalm 37:23**

How would you define the word decision? Think about some of the past decisions you have made! And their consequences! Here is an internet definition: *"A conclusion or resolution reached after consideration."* Here are some similar words: resolution, conclusion, settlement, commitment, determination, choice, option, selection, judgment, decree, order, finding, rule, resolution, etc. God uses such words to make his points. The word decree is used 55 times in the Bible. Look at God's use of decree in **Job 22:28**:

"Thou shalt also <u>decree</u> a thing, and it shall be established unto thee: and the light shall shine upon thy ways."

I love to use such authority while praying about a particular matter in the power of **Phillippians 2:10**. It is more likely my prayer will actually affect change in a situation I am concerned about. I have seen God change many situations after I prayed using his authority.

early life decisions

Have you purposed in your heart to be a good person? At a very early age, I had a desire in me to please my parents. I was not a rebellious child. I don't know where this desire to please my parents came from. I do not see such a desire inherent in some small children. Why can one child have such a desire, and another be so difficult right out of the womb? I think it must have come about that I was an easy child when I was young because someone was praying for me in the family. Most likely a parent, grandparent, or great grandparent who knew the value of prayer.

For twenty plus years, I went to a Christian men's camp at Fort Flagler on the Olympic Peninsula in Washington State. It had to close a few years ago as it became too difficult to stay open. What a blessing it was to be with like-minded men who knew the value of prayer.

One of the men who also attended started a smaller camp of about fifteen men on southern Washington on a river. He is a man of vision and prayer and invites Christian men. He has a heart for Israel and has made over twelve trips there to intercede. I am looking forward to seeing what the Lord is saying to these men in June 2021.

God gave me a one-word quest after I closed my website in 2018 and asked Him what next: *"millennials."* With this answer, I decided to do some research. This led to my writing a program (draft) to help struggling millennials in small towns across America. I have not done anything to implement this program: it would be expensive. And the situation spelled out in **II Timothy 3** is, I believe. About this struggling generation, God led me to focus on. I have not been given the funds necessary to proceed, even with a pilot test so far. So the research I have done is in the hands of the LORD. I did talk to one city administrator of a small, nearby town. She encouraged me. She has some millennials inside her extended family as well.

When I prayed and asked the Lord what next, and when I felt I had heard the Lord's answer, I decided to do that research. When anyone in a family is struggling, it affects the entire family and the neighborhood and community where that family resides, especially after that child becomes an adult and does not lead a productive life. Living at home off one's parent's generosity is not good.

age of accountability

When we are young, we are molded deliberately or maybe through neglect into young adults. At some point, we are expected by society to venture out on our own. The profitable opinions and beliefs of those who raised us should become our own unless we are rebellious. According to the Bible, those attitudes, opinions, and values that are unrighteous put us on a path towards hell.

"Enter ye in at the strait gate: for wide is the gate, and broad is the way that leadeth to destruction, and many there be which go in thereat: Because strait is the gate, and narrow is the way which leadeth unto

life, and few there be that find it." ~**Matthew 7:13-14**

At some point, we should become accountable for our actions and decisions, even while living at home! But certainly, after moving out! Once out on our own, we need to take a hard look at ourselves and the way we think.

"Examine yourselves, whether ye be in the faith; prove your own selves, know ye, not your own selves, how that Jesus Christ, is in you, except ye be reprobates?" ~**II Corinthians 13:5**

Are you really happy with the way things are going? Who are you, and what are you becoming? Listen to yourself closely when you are thinking, speaking, and pondering. Examine who you are from what others seem to think of you when around you. We all need to make certain changes if we are honest with ourselves. How happy are you with the way our country is going? What are you doing as a citizen to affect others? Do you vote? Is yours really an informed vote? Many do not really see the depth of division in our nation or which side they should be on in the current struggle.

exceptional nation

I have studied the history of warfare and civilization. The attacks that have been waged against America and how far we have fallen below God's standard in my lifetime amazes me. The below quote was put in the Congressional Record. It was written in 1965. This was the year my regiment deployed to Vietnam.

if I were the devil

If I were the devil ... I would gain control of the most powerful nation in the world;

I would delude their minds into thinking that they had come from man's effort, instead of God's blessings;

I would promote an attitude of loving things and using people, instead of the other way around;

I would dupe entire states into relying on gambling
for their state revenue;

I would convince people that character is not an issue
when it comes to leadership;

I would make it legal to take the life of unborn
babies;

I would make it socially acceptable to take one's own
life and invent machines to make it convenient;

I would cheapen human life as much as possible so
that the life of animals are valued more than human beings;

I would take God out of the schools, where even the
mention of His name was grounds for a lawsuit;

I would come up with drugs that sedate the mind and
target the young, and I would get sports heroes to advertise
them;

I would get control of the media so that every night I
could pollute the mind of every family member for my
agenda;

I would attack the family, the backbone of any nation.

I would make divorce acceptable and easy, even
fashionable. If the family crumbles, so does the nation;

I would compel people to express their most depraved
fantasies on canvas and movie screens, and I would call it
art;

I would convince the world that people are born
homosexuals and that their lifestyles should be accepted and
marveled;

209

I would convince the people that right and wrong are determined by a few who call themselves authorities and refer to their agenda as politically correct;

I would persuade people that the church is irrelevant and out of date, and the Bible is for the naive;

I would dull the minds of Christians and make them believe that prayer is not important, and that faithfulness and obedience are optional;

I guess I would leave things pretty much the way they are. ~**Paul Harvey**

worse still

Are things in your view getting better or worse in our nation and the world? People seem almost equally divided on what is going on and whose fault it is. Millennials grew up in an age that was not of their choosing. Things moved along at a much slower pace in the 1950s when I was coming of age as a high schooler. My focus was more on personal achievement growing up. I was not raised in the era of smartphones, thank God. The situation is so different now: especially in terms of outside distractions such as living on FACEBOOK.

We don't have to go back very far! Many are still alive who lived before the age of jets and before removing Christian prayer from the public schools! Before abortion became legal! Before the age of no-fault divorce! Before the age of computers and transgenderism! I have lived through massive social change. And this change is accelerating! Much of it not good! What is normal these days was not normal when I was young. The genie has been let out of the bottle. And there is no going back to simpler, more righteous times. So how do we cope if we are somewhat normal? How do we exist in an age gone mad? This is an important question to ask. Your children are being taught in public schools things that go against your sacred beliefs.

normalcy bias

Normalcy bias is *"a belief people hold when there is a possibility of a disaster. It causes people to underestimate both the likelihood of a disaster and its possible effects because people believe that things will always function the way things normally have functioned."* Wikipedia

People believe it is critical to make their way through life in the face of the growing list of obstacles to good living and still make healthy decisions. In discussing strategy, I would have liked to talk about the direct versus the indirect approach to achieve an important objective. Biblical prophecy tells us the craziness we are seeing will get worse. Things will not get better: only worse. You will never see normal again on this side of heaven. How do we cope with this growing reality concerning what is real and what is not real, but an illusion? Denial is not the answer. We must decide to bring God more into our life, to pray more, to throw ourselves on his mercy, and to believe what he says and tells us to do.

and they think we are crazy

Most accusations from the MSM continue to be pointed at the righteous, not the guilty. Why? Lying and accusing one's opponents sways the gullible and simple-minded. Even if we are innocent when we are accused, a lot of trouble still comes our way. Liars verbally abuse us to take the focus off themselves. We know they are wrong and wonder why others cannot see this. Their unjust verbal barbs hurt and sway the double-minded and naive toward giving in to their point of view. As wrong as it is: *"The squeaky wheel does get the grease."* We cannot win the argument in the natural realm. Most of us are living a somewhat normal life and do not have the time, energy, talent, or finances to fight evil doers in court. They know this. When the truth is on our side, we must decide to fight them when, where, and how we can, if we can. The final victory, if we do not quit, is promised to us by God.

the power of decrees

God's ways are higher than man's ways. He has all power in heaven and on earth and below. So:

"Thou shalt also decree a thing, and it shall be established unto thee: and the light shall shine upon thy ways." ~Job 22:28

How can we be sure God is on our side in a dispute? Well! Have you repented? Have you forgiven? Have you taken the matter to God in prayer? Then you will know when you are in God's will. Are you praying in righteousness to your Heavenly Father in Jesus Christ's Name? Have you elicited help from one or two strong, mature believers to agree with you in prayer? How about the gift of tongues? Have you discovered the power of tongues yet? That is how you get the Holy Spirit moving on your behalf in a dispute. Let him pray through you!

"For if I pray in an unknown tongue, my spirit prayeth, but my understanding is unfruitful."
~I Corinthians 14:14

If you do not want to just depend on the Holy Ghost on how it comes out, then ask for and contend for the interpretation of tongues, another gift. But stay in faith and increase the amount of time you pray in the Spirit, in tongues, until the answer or interpretation comes. Personally, I pray in tongues more than most I know. I do not say this to brag but to share its importance. I have just found it works for me. It is a passion of mine. At my age, I walk in health; few seem to enjoy and have need of nothing personally.

nothing impossible with God

"For with God nothing shall be impossible," so says
Luke 1:37: but do you really deep down believe it?

In seeing God work, it is all about identity. Is your
identity hidden in Christ or not? When we surrender our life to
Jesus Christ, there is a cloak of invincibility that comes with a
true surrender. When we take our eyes off ourselves and put
them on him, everything begins to change for the better. Satan
is not afraid of us, but He is afraid of God Almighty. That is
why we pray to our Father in his Son's Mighty Name. A gifted
teacher, Dr. Kevin Zadai, talks about the secret place. He says
when we place our faith in God and not in ourselves and other
created beings, and our faith starts to grow, it starts extending
beyond ourselves and affects the spirit realm. The demons just
start to leave the space where our faith reaches. He says a lot of
things that have been said as well or better by others.

I love Evangelist Norvel Hayes. I had personally heard
him speak on matters of faith in the late 1970s and early 80s
when he came to Warm Beach Campgrounds and spoke at
F.GM.M.F.I. meetings north of Seattle. A powerful man of
God! A great storyteller!

I was trained to use many of the power tools available
to the United States Marine Corps in warfighting operations.
But I have to tell you; they don't work against Satan's demonic
forces as well without prayer. They certainly are effective
against people on the Darkside, even those skilled in
witchcraft. But practice in both realms is critical to success.
Laziness is not rewarded.

Demon inspired men are no match for believers who
are empowered by God. But we must use the weapons God
tells us to use in the Bible. I grew up believing in the Father,
the Son, and the Holy Spirit in a religious way. I believed in
prayer but only knew a little. There was so much more I needed
to know. My spiritual understanding was weak because of a

lack of spiritual knowledge and not being born again or filled with the Spirit in earlier life. The power of the Holy Spirit was not understood by most around me, so how could I know. Many of my teachers thought good people were spiritually blind to some of the things of God. If I was protected, it was more likely God's grace in operation. Since my dramatic encounter with Jesus in 1978, I have been reading the Bible, where my understanding really took off. What a privilege to watch him for over 50 minutes as he interceded for us from Heaven! What power he projected in all directions, like bolts of lightning, as he prayed for his church on earth.

"Wherefore, he is able also to save them to the uttermost that come unto God by him, seeing he ever liveth to make intercession for them." ~**Hebrews 7:25**

15

WATCHING

Early this morning (Friday, December 20, 2019), I was half-awake. Hanukkah came to my mind. I thought could it be rapture time? When I got up, I checked my computer to see what I had concerning this feast. A posting from the five Dove's website was in my file from Lisa Taylor. She wondered if the rapture might be on Hanukkah. The rapture didn't occur. She never claimed to be a prophet, just a watcher. Like her, I, too, am a watcher. I do not claim to have any great seer skills. I just try to stay current on the national and international news in light of the clear teachings of scripture, especially prophecy. Most believers are too busy with their lives or distracted to stay alert, so some look to watchers to stay aware. Watching requires time, and few have much of that commodity as they struggle to make a living and cope with the everyday problems all busy people have. The scary thing is that so few even seem to care about prophecy or the importance of watching.

I have written about why this is likely the generation that will experience the rapture. Those who are left behind will experience the resulting seven years of tribulation. Much has been written about it in various books of the Bible. Frankly, few local churches I am aware of in my community seem to concern themselves with what is going on beyond their local church doors. This is not wise in light of the clear warnings in scripture. Many kind, decent people are fast asleep concerning what has been prophesized and is quite likely to happen very soon. Look at the sum of the Drudge Report Headlines below for January 3, 2020. The new year got off with a bang in light of prophecy.

The Iranian general who was killed was looked upon by some as a likely candidate for the coming antichrist. He is no more. He was a hero in Islam. Repercussions were expected.

Trump Rattles Mideast with Risky Strike...
Soleimani 'torn to shreds' by missile...
Body identified by ring...
DRONES FOUND HIM...
Pentagon says was planning new attacks...
Assassination triggers global alarm...

And then the release of the Covid-19 pandemic! Was this China's first shot fired in the start of WWIII? I don't know, but it seems likely. If it is true divine protection will be needed at the individual and family level more than ever. This book is not intended to be a definitive work on Spiritual Warfare. My purpose is to highlight the importance of reading scripture daily. There are more comprehensive published works on the basics of spiritual warfare elsewhere. They give more details. I want to keep this short but impactful. I want to motivate believers to become more aware. The church must understand the watchers' essential functions and not overlook them as most churches seem to do. Every extended family needs someone willing to study the subject of spiritual warfare. It is very important for survival in times of tribulation.

I address this subject not as a pastor, teacher, evangelist, prophet, or apostle. But as a husband, father, layman, watcher, and as one born into and raised in the military culture. I was a professional warfighter for a long season of my life. This work provides a different slant on this subject than I have seen before. I hope it proves to be a book you want to keep close at hand. It should lead to some eye-opening discussions if you share with family and friends.

My wife and I are parents, grandparents, and great-grandparents. We were involved in the healing room's movement that originated in Spokane, Washington, and served seven years at the Yakima Healing Center run by Paul and Beth Stadler. This started back up long after the death of John G. Lake, who originated this movement. Signs and wonders followed his teachings in the early 20th Century. He was a great man of God! God used him powerfully in healing and deliverance through the power of the Holy Ghost. Karen and I also went into the Yakima Jail weekly for six years, helping incarcerated women. We have personally experienced signs and wonders following our teachings. Ours is a second marriage. We have nine married children between the two of us. Karen has five. I have four.

We believe God's healing and deliverance power are available to all who truly believe. The leaders of the established church, it clearly tells us in the Book of Ephesians, are *"to equip the saints for the work of the ministry."* This has not been done effectively in many churches now dead or dying. The pews today are full of spectators watching the few professionals attempting to put on a good show. The clergy works while most of the laity watch and help by financing the professionals. This is why there is so little power in most churches today. Thank God for good done by the few, of course. Many church members are outside the church building all week in a world that does not know Christ, and political correctness has shut many down as witnesses.

the harvest is ripe, the laborers few

Jesus Christ came to Israel. Most missed that visitation. He returned to heaven. The Father sent the Holy Spirit. Many churches today have a corporate style of leadership, which is mostly about growing the church! The Holy Ghost can't be managed. The Holy Ghost gifts, such as tongues and interpretation, healing and miracles, and deliverance, can't be supervised. So these precious gifts are unknown to many. Heaven, hell, sin, real evil, devils and prophecy, the rapture, tribulation, and the second coming are glossed over or ignored by some leaders as too controversial. And there is little understanding of spiritual warfare. I see in scripture that Jesus Christ is a warfighter and came to destroy the enemy's works. A real Christian soldier should not shy away from the call to battle.

It will take more than China, Iran, and their proxies to bring America down. Unless, of course, we help them from within, which many citizens are now doing. Hamstringing Christianity and throwing open the doors to Islam seems insane, but we see it happening. Look at what such immigration has done to Europe. The Muslims I have met are very nice. I have ministered the gospel in Russia. I really liked the Russian people. Like here in America, it is those who seek secular power that appears to me to be the main problem. Most people are friendly that I have met in other nations.

In light of the absence of America in Bible prophecy and having studied prophesy seriously, I want readers to know that we need watchers to sound the alarm when they see the enemy at hand. Missing the next visitation of God to earth will be costly to those left behind. The consequences of that tragedy for them and their families in light of clear teaching in the Bible will be horrific.

exhortation to watch

"But of that day and that hour knoweth no man, no, not the angels which are in heaven, neither the Son, but the Father. Take ye heed, <u>watch</u> and pray for ye know not when the time is. For the Son of man is as a man taking a far journey, who left his house, and gave authority to his servants, and to every man, his work and commanded the porter to <u>watch</u>. <u>Watch</u> ye therefore: for ye know not when the master of the house cometh, at even, or at midnight, or at the cockcrowing, or in the morning: Lest coming suddenly he find you sleeping. And what I say unto you I say unto all, <u>Watch</u>." **Mark 13:32-37, KJV**

"Let your loins be girded about, and your lights burning; And ye yourselves like unto men that wait for their lord, when he will return from the wedding; that when he cometh and knocketh, they may open unto him immediately. Blessed are those servants, whom the lord when he cometh shall find <u>watching</u>: verily I say unto you, that he shall gird himself, and make them to sit down to meat, and will come forth and serve them. And if he shall come in the second watch, or come in the third watch, and find them so, blessed are those servants. And this know, that if the goodman of the house had known what hour the thief would come, he would have <u>watched</u>, and not have suffered his house to be broken through. Be ye, therefore, ready also: for the Son of man cometh at an hour when ye think not." **Luke 12:35-40, KJV**

"Remember therefore how thou hast received and heard, and hold fast, and repent. If therefore thou shalt not <u>watch</u>, I will come on thee as a thief, and thou shalt not know what hour I will come upon thee." **Revelation 3:3, KJV**

I will begin closing this book with a warning from a great American:

the Prophecy of George Washington

"Washington's Vision" is a narrative presented as the 1859 reminiscences of 99-year-old Anthony Sherman, who was reportedly present with George Washington's army at Valley Forge during the winter of 1777. He overheard Washington tell an officer that an angel had revealed a prophetic vision of America to him. The passage of more than 150 years has obscured the origin and purpose of this narrative. Many who hear of it believe that it is a true account of an incident from Washington's life. It was published in the Armed Forces Stars and Stripes Newspaper in 1950 during the Korea War. It was also published in its forerunner during the Civil War. Some suggest it is a fictional tale created for political purposes long after Washington's death. It shows three perils that will come upon America. If true, it steeled Washington showing him the outcome of the Revolutionary War he was then fighting. It showed the outcome of the next war also: the bloody American Civil War. It also shows the outcome of the last war to be fought on America's soil. We seem to be in such a time right now: An indirect war being fought mostly out of public view. Will it become more conventional with actual attacks from hostile nations? Will we be judged as a sheep nation or a goat nation when Jesus Christ returns at his second coming to the earth to rule and reign one thousand years? I prayed President Trump and a spirit of righteousness would turn this nation around. I would hate to see us become part of the one-world government ruled by the anti-Christ for seven years, which those in the deep state are actively attempting to bring about behind the scenes here in America.

the future president's vision

"The last time I ever saw Anthony Sherman was on the Fourth of July 1859, in Independence Square. He was then ninety-nine years old; his dimming eyes rekindled as he gazed upon Independence Hall, which he had come to visit once more. "I want to tell you an incident of Washington's

life one which no one alive knows of except myself; and which, if you live, you will before long see verified."

He said, "From the opening of the Revolution, we experienced all phases of fortune, good and ill. The darkest period we ever had, I think, was when Washington, after several reverses, retreated to Valley Forge, where he resolved to pass the winter of 1777. Ah! I often saw the tears coursing down our dear commander's careworn cheeks as he conversed with a confidential officer about the condition of his soldiers. You have doubtless heard the story of Washington's going to the thicket to pray. Well, he also used to pray to God in secret for aid and comfort.

"One day, I remember well, the chilly winds whistled through the leafless trees. Though the sky was cloudless, and the sun shone brightly, he remained alone in his quarters nearly all afternoon. When he came out, I noticed that his face was a shade paler than usual, and there seemed to be something on his mind of more than ordinary importance. Returning just after dusk, he dispatched an orderly to the quarters of the officer I mentioned who was in attendance at the time. After a preliminary conversation of about half an hour, Washington, gazing upon his companion with that strange look of dignity that he alone could command, said to the latter:

"I do not know whether it is due to the anxiety of my mind or what, but this afternoon, as I was preparing a dispatch, something seemed to disturb me. Looking up, I beheld, standing opposite me, a singularly beautiful being. So astonished was I, for I had given strict orders not to be disturbed, that it was some moments before I found language to inquire the cause of the visit. A second, a third, and even a fourth time did I repeat my question but received no answer from my mysterious visitor, except a slight raising of the eyes. By this time, I felt strange sensations spreading through me, and I would have risen, but the riveted gaze of the being before me rendered volition impossible. I assayed once more

221

to speak, but my tongue had become useless, as though it had become paralyzed. A new influence, mysterious, potent, irresistible, took possession. All I could do was to gaze steadily, vacantly at my unknown visitor. Gradually the surrounding atmosphere seemed to become filled with sensations and grew luminous. Everything about me seemed to rarefy, including the mysterious visitor.

"I began to feel as one dying, or rather to experience the sensations which I have sometimes imagined accompany dissolution. I did not think; I did not reason; I did not move; all were alike impossible. I was only conscious of gazing fixedly, vacantly at my companion.

"Presently I heard a voice saying, 'Son of the Republic, look and learn,' while at the same time my visitor extended an arm eastwardly. I now beheld a heavy vapor at some distance rising fold upon fold. This gradually dissipated, and I looked out upon a strange scene. Before me lay spread out in one vast plain all the countries of the world — Europe, Asia, Africa, and America. I saw rolling and tossing between Europe and America the billows of the Atlantic, and between Asia and America lay the Pacific.

" 'Son of the Republic,' said the same mysterious voice as before, 'look and learn.' At that moment, I beheld a dark, shadowy being as an angel standing, or rather floating, in mid-air between Europe and America. Dipping water out of the ocean in the hollow of his hand, he cast some on Europe. Immediately a cloud raised from these countries and joined in mid-ocean. For a while, it remained stationary and then moved slowly westward until it enveloped America in its murky folds. Sharp flashes of lightning gleamed through it at intervals, and I heard the smothered groans and cries of the American people. A second time the angel dipped water from the ocean and sprinkled it out as before. The dark cloud was then drawn back to the ocean, in whose billows it sank from view.

"A third time I heard the mysterious voice saying, 'Son of the Republic, look and learn.' I cast my eyes upon America and beheld villages and towns and cities string up one after another until the whole landform the Atlantic to the Pacific was dotted with them. Again, I heard the mysterious voice say, 'Son of the Republic, the end of the century cometh; look and learn.'

"And this time the dark, shadowy angel turned his face southward, and from Africa, I saw an ill-omened specter approach our land. It flitted slowly over every town and city of the latter. The inhabitants presently set themselves in a battle against each other. As I continued looking, I saw a bright angel, on whose brow rested a crown of light on which was traced the word 'Union,' bearing the American flag, which he placed between the divided nation. He said, 'Remember, ye are brethren.' Instantly the inhabitants, casting down their weapons, became friends once more and united around the National Standard.

Again, I heard the mysterious voice saying, 'Son of the Republic, look and learn.' At this, the dark, shadowy angel placed a trumpet to his lips and blew three distinct blasts; and taking water from the ocean, he sprinkled it on Europe, Asia, and Africa. Then my eyes beheld a fearful scene. From each of these countries arose thick black clouds that were soon joined into one; and throughout this mass there gleamed a dark red light be which I saw hordes of armed men, who, moving with the cloud, marched by land, and sailed by sea to America, which country was enveloped in the volume of cloud. And I dimly saw these vast armies devastate the whole country and burn the villages, towns, and cities that I had beheld springing up.

As my ears listened to the thundering of the cannon, the slashing of swords, and the shouts and cries of millions in mortal combat, I again heard the mysterious voice saying, 'Son of the Republic, look and learn.' When the voice had ceased, the dark angel placed his trumpet once more to his mouth and blew a long and fearful blast.

"Instantly a light as of a thousand suns shown down from above me, and pierced and broke into fragments the dark cloud which enveloped America. At the same moment, the angel upon whose head still shown the word 'Union' and who bore our national flag in one hand and a sword in the other descended from the heavens attended by legions of white spirits. These immediately joined the inhabitants of America, who I perceived were well-nigh overcome, but who, immediately taking courage again, closed up their broken ranks and renewed the battle. Again, amid the fearful noise of the conflict, I heard the mysterious voice saying, 'Son of the Republic, look and learn.' As the voice ceased, the shadowy angel for the last time dipped water from the ocean and sprinkled it upon America. Instantly the dark cloud rolled back, together with the armies it had brought, leaving the inhabitants of the land victorious.

"Then once more, I beheld the villages, towns, and cities springing up where I'd seen them before, while the bright angel, planting the azure standard he had brought in the midst of them, cried with a loud voice: 'While the stars remain, and the heavens send down dew upon the earth, so long shall the Union last.' And taking from his brow the crown on which blazoned the word 'Union,' he placed it upon the standard while the people, kneeling down, said 'Amen.'

The scene instantly began to fade and dissolve, and I, at last, saw nothing but the rising, curling vapor I had at first beheld. This also disappeared, and I found myself once more gazing upon the mysterious visitor, who in the same voice I had heard before said, 'Son of the Republic, what you have seen is thus interpreted. Three great perils will come upon the Republic. The most fearful is the third, but in this greatest conflict the whole world united shall not prevail against her. Let every child of the Republic learn to live for his God, his land, and the Union.' With these words, the vision vanished,

*and I started from my seat and felt that I had seen a vision
wherein had been shown me the birth, progress, and destiny
of the United States."*

*"Such, my friends," said the venerable narrator,
"were the words I heard from Washington's own lips, and
America will do well to profit by them."*

The tale of "Washington's Vision" was written down
by Charles Wesley Alexander (1836-1927), a Philadelphia
journalist who published The Soldier's Casket, a periodical
for Union veterans of the Civil War. Did he hear this tale
from one who had been with the general? Or was it fiction?
Either way, it seems prophetic to me in light of today's
headlines and the increasingly unfriendly struggle between
liberals and conservatives presently in progress. Both Antifa
and BLM movements are increasingly communist and hostile
to law and order. Communists have overcome many nations
by doing just as we are watching them do right now.

*"But of that day and hour knoweth no man, no, not
the angels of heaven, but my Father only. But as the days of
Noe were, so shall also the coming of the Son of man be. For
as in the days that were before the flood they were eating and
drinking, marrying and giving in marriage, until the day that
Noe entered into the ark, and knew not until the flood came,
and took them all away; so shall also the coming of the Son of
man be. Then shall two be in the field; the one shall be taken,
and the other left. Two women shall be grinding at the mill;
the one shall be taken, and the other left. Watch therefore: for
ye know not what hour your Lord doth come. But know this,
that if the goodman of the house had known in what watch the
thief would come, he would have watched and would not have
suffered his house to be broken up. Therefore, be ye also
ready: for in such an hour as ye think not the Son of man
cometh. Who then is a faithful and wise servant, whom his
lord hath made ruler over his household, to give them meat in
due season? Blessed is that servant, whom his lord when he
cometh shall find so doing. Verily I say unto you, That he*

shall make him ruler over all his goods. "
~**Matthew 24:36-47, KJV**

16

HISTORY REPEATS

An understanding of history is critical. People must see where unrighteousness takes a nation. Most students graduating today from high schools have a pitiful understanding of history. Is this on purpose? In large, our education system seems to have replaced history with political correctness and sex education. Hopefully, Betsy DeBois did something about this. Those who study history have read the quote that: *"Those who do not learn history are doomed to repeat it."* It probably came from Philosopher George Santayana. He said this about human nature: *"Only the dead have seen the end of war."* He died in Rome six years before I graduated high school in 1958. This last chapter will share some closing thoughts about what the Bible tells us is coming.

prophecy is future history

There is a point coming in history where the rebel against God runs out of time:

He that is unjust let him be unjust still: and he which is filthy, let him be filthy still: and he that is righteous, let him be righteous still: and he that is holy, let him be holy still. And behold, I come quickly; and my reward is with me, to give every man according as his work shall be.~ ***Revelations 22:11-12***

Whether one believes the Bible and this verse are the inerrant words of God, there are eternal consequences that come with free will. I do not put the same confidence in George Washington's Prophecy I do in the sacred scriptures. But it seems to line up with actual history and the Bible remarkably well.

Our first president, it is recorded, was a man of prayer. Two-thirds of this vision has already happened since his experience at Valley Forge that terrible winter day of the vision. I do believe God would put steel into the General's resolve for our sakes by telling him the outcome of our nation's struggle to survive the British. "God does speak to men through dreams and visions."

Is it true an attack on the United States is in our future? Much good fiction has been written about WWIII. It will be an awful time. A quarter to half the world population is expected to perish if one believes **the Book of Revelation.** This is what God tells us is coming.

divine favor

There are five verses in Scripture that refer to Israel as the apple of God's eye. If the United States has any such favor, it is only because of those who are righteous in God's eyes who dwell in our midst. If and when the rapture occurs, or the majority turn against these righteous ones, God will write Icabode on our leaders' heads and certainly depart as he did the ancient nation of Israel before its destruction.

Alexis de Tocqueville, a famous 19th-century French statesman, historian, and social philosopher, traveled to America in the 1830s. He wanted to discover the reasons for the incredible success of America. He published his observations in a classic two-volume work: Democracy in America. He was especially impressed with America's religious character. Here are some startling excerpts:

"Upon my arrival in the United States, the religious aspect of the country was the first thing that struck my attention. The longer I stayed there, the more I perceived the great political consequences resulting from this new state of things.

In France, I had almost always seen the spirit of religion and the spirit of freedom marching in opposite directions. In America, I found they were intimately united and that they reigned in common over the same country.

Religion in America...must be regarded as the foremost of the political institutions of that country; for if it does not impart a taste for freedom, it facilitates the use of it. Indeed, it is in this same point of view that the inhabitants of the United States themselves look upon religious belief.

I do not know whether all Americans have a sincere faith in their religion -- for who can search the human heart? But I am certain that they hold it to be indispensable to the maintenance of republican institutions. This opinion is not peculiar to a class of citizens or a party, but it belongs to the whole nation and to every rank of society.

In the United States, the sovereign authority is religious...there is no country in the world where the Christian religion retains a greater influence over the souls of men than in America, and there can be no greater proof of its utility and of its conformity to human nature than that its influence is powerfully felt over the most enlightened and free nation of the earth.

In the United States, the influence of religion is not confined to the manners, but it extends to the intelligence of the people...

Christianity, therefore, reigns without obstacle, by universal consent...

I sought for the key to the greatness and genius of America in her harbors...; in her fertile fields and boundless forests; in her rich mines and vast world commerce; in her public school system and institutions of learning. I sought for it in her democratic Congress and in her matchless Constitution.

Not until I went into the churches of America and heard her pulpits flame with righteousness did, I understand the secret of her genius and power.

America is great because America is good, and if America ever ceases to be good, America will cease to be great.

The safeguard of morality is religion, and morality is the best security of law as well as the surest pledge of freedom.

The Americans combine the notions of Christianity and of liberty so intimately in their minds that it is impossible to make them conceive the one without the other

Christianity is the companion of liberty in all its conflicts -- the cradle of its infancy, and the divine source of its claims. "

Tocqueville gives this account of a court case in New York:

"While I was in America, a witness, who happened to be called at the assizes of the county of Chester (state of New York), declared that he did not believe in the existence of God or in the immortality of the soul. The judge refused to admit his evidence, on the ground that the witness had destroyed beforehand all confidence of the court in what he was about to say. The newspapers related the fact without any further comment. The New York Spectator of August 23rd, 1831, relates the fact in the following terms:

"The court of common pleas of Chester county (New York), a few days since rejected a witness who declared his disbelief in the existence of God. The presiding judge remarked that he had not before been aware that there was a man living who did not believe in the existence of God; that this belief constituted the sanction of all testimony in a court of justice: and that he knew of no case in a Christian country, where a witness had been permitted to testify without such belief."

are we still exceptional

These observations of Alexis de Tocqueville are shocking in light of America in 2021. He would be astounded by our decline if he could come back from the dead for another visit.

Ancient Israel made some grave mistakes. Their worst mistake, in my view, was that they missed the time of their visitation (**Luke 19:44**). By this, I mean very few Jews in the light of what their prophets had foretold recognized or received their Messiah when he visited them 2,000 years ago. There are fifteen verses of scripture that warn people of what happens when they miss the time of their visitation. Jesus said this:

"And when he was come near, he beheld the city, and wept over it, Saying, If thou hadst known, even thou, at least in this thy day, the things which belong unto thy peace! But now they are hid from thine eyes. For the days shall come upon thee, that thine enemies shall cast a trench about thee, and compass thee round, and keep thee in on every side, And shall lay thee even with the ground, and thy children within thee; and they shall not leave in thee one stone upon another; because thou knewest not the time of thy visitation." ~**Luke 19:42-44**

Here in America, many churches reject the Holy Ghost in the same way Jesus Christ was rejected 2,000 years ago by Israel. I saw a recent study that only two percent of local church sermons have any prophetic content at all. Yet one-third of the Bible is prophetic. As I reflect back over the years and years of Sunday sermons I have listened to, this reflects my experience also. I am sad to say this: as the "watchman" in my family. I raised my children in the church. I depended on the pastor's help to give them the truth. Most unintentionally let me down prophetically. Now that I am aware, my children are long gone from my home with their own opinions.

There are over 30 references to the importance of the word *"watchman"* in the Bible. I know very few, personally, that are interested in prophecy. Not one pastor in a church I was attending my first 40 years had any real understanding of the importance of prophecy at least that they shared Sunday mornings.

I now look daily at the news in light of Bible prophecy. I research to inform myself of any new spiritual insights in light of scripture. For instance, a loose movement called: "The New Apostolic Reformation." Many who love Christ are not aware of this movement affecting the church. I think of what Martin Luther and other reformers achieved 500 years ago. They turned the world upside down. But these new reformers are politically correct. Not good! Having studied the

New Age secular movement, I would say there is a danger this is its spiritual cousin.

a nation's protection

Why I find Tocqueville's assessment of America in the 1800s so interesting is because the nation has strayed so far from his recognition of the importance of our moral underpinnings. That visit from a knowledgeable Frenchman was only about 200 years ago. How far we have fallen spiritually is shocking. It is one great indication that the point of our nation's visitation from God is very near. The Bible makes this so clear to those who just are not picking and choosing what to believe from the Bible.

*" Some trust in chariots and some in horses: but we will remember the name of the LORD our God."~ **Psalms 20:7***

In my lifetime, I have seen our nation grow weaker in the only area that really matters. When the "chips are down:" it's moral character that will matter. The church I know is now fragile compared to when I was a younger man. It was not as blind in the area of prophecy as now. I do not sense the Holy Ghost much in church activities anymore. Most citizens have no idea biblically of what is prophesized to come suddenly and unexpectedly upon this nation and the world. I seriously wonder, in light of scripture, if our talented past President Trump will be able to turn things around a second time, at least morally. The genie has been let out of the bottle. I do think his personal angel might be the one spoken of by our founder, George Washington, as the Angel of the Union.

the rise and fall of civilizations

There are different ways to look at the rise and fall of empires. In studying civilizations while on a three-year military teaching assignment, one of the first studies I found teaching the history of warfare at the University of Washington occurred about the time our original 13 states adopted their new constitution. In 1787, Alexander Tyler, a Scottish history professor at the University of Edinburgh, had this to say about the fall of the Athenian Republic 2000 years prior:

"A democracy is always temporary in nature; it simply cannot exist as a permanent form of government. A democracy will continue to exist up until the time that voters discover they can vote themselves generous gifts from the public treasury. From that moment on, the majority always votes for the candidates who promise the most benefits from the public treasury, with the result that every democracy will finally collapse due to loose fiscal policy, which is always followed by a dictatorship."

"The average age of the world's greatest civilizations from the beginning of history has been about 200 years. During those 200 years, these nations always progressed through the following sequence:

1. From bondage to spiritual faith;
2. From spiritual faith to great courage;
3. From courage to liberty;
4. From liberty to abundance;
5. From abundance to complacency;
6. From complacency to apathy;
7. From apathy to dependence;
8. From dependence back into bondage."

what stage are we in

I see a lot of complacency, apathy, insecurity, and dependency here in America. At one time, we were an exceptional nation. I do not see this so clearly anymore. Another way of looking at the timing of what is happening in our country is a concept I recently ran across titled the Four Waves. I saw it on the internet; no name was attached to the originator in that article.

"First the dreamers come, followed by the builders, then the eaters and finally those who are discontent bringing about destruction."

I see a definite increase in what communists call useless eaters who appear not to be motivated to contribute in any useful manner to our society. There are increasing numbers of angry complainers with almost nothing good to say. Too many are just complaining and expecting handouts showing no appreciation. What some do best, it seems, is looking for freebies. How do we get such people motivated? I have been looking at studies and scripture to inform myself. What can I personally do to help offset these worrisome trends in my little community? Certainly, I do pray. And I have written an S.O.P. for millennials that sits on a shelf because I don't have the money to fund even one pilot study to see if it can help a small town. And I write letters to the Editor of the local paper.

praying God's word

"All scripture is given by inspiration of God, and is profitable for doctrine, for reproof, for correction, for instruction in righteousness: That the man of God may be perfect, thoroughly furnished unto all good works."~ II Timothy 3:15-17

" According as his divine power hath given unto us all things that pertain unto life and godliness, through the knowledge of him that hath called us to glory and virtue: Whereby are given unto us exceeding great and precious promises: that by these ye might be partakers of the divine nature, having escaped the corruption that is in the world through lust." ~
~II Peter 1:3-4

divine benefits

I found from talking to those who love God that many are not aware they have been given a supernatural benefits package when they surrendered their lives to our Heavenly Father. They are not aware that when they appropriated what Jesus Christ died for them at the cross, it really affects their personal daily living. The word "benefits" is found eight times in my Bible. Let us look at just a couple of verses.

"Bless the LORD, O my soul, and forget not all his benefits, who forgives all your iniquity, who heals all your diseases, who redeems your life from the pit, who crowns you with steadfast love and mercy, who satisfies you with good so that your youth is renewed like the eagles.~Psalms 103: 2-5

"Blessed be the Lord, who daily loadeth us with benefits, even the God of our salvation. Selah. He that is our God is the God of salvation, and unto GOD, the Lord belong the issues from death. But God shall wound the head of his enemies, and the hairy scalp of such a one as goeth on still in his trespasses." ~Psalms 68:19-21

I like sharing such verses with those who need divine help in their life. I have found that few are really aware of what God really wants to do for his family on earth. We know how he promises to take care of his family and friends who have died and are now in heaven. We should await that time confident of his goodness. But what about here on earth right now? Many who confess Christ struggle while here. If they are aware of these benefits that have accrued to them as believers in Jesus Christ, many seem not able to appropriate them. They do look to government benefits and insurance benefits from the fruits of their labors. But not so much to God for help. Yes, they do send up the occasional prayer for help when things become desperate! But have they really looked at the divine benefits that are theirs in this world?

For much of my life, I was not really aware of them myself. When I became aware, I didn't really know how to appropriate them. Or who was working to keep me from acquiring them! We are in a battle. We need our Heavenly Father's help. Why? Because our primary enemies are supernatural entities!

past and future visitations

The word "visitation" is so important to study. It is a key study for a watcher like me. Such knowledge keeps me motivated and bold. Prophets and Jesus Christ have suffered trying to get this important word into our hands. Prophecy speaks of past and future judgments that have or will happen.

When Jesus Christ came at his first official visit to earth, we see how he was treated and what happened within a few years after his departure back to Heaven. We learn in the gospel story of the Father's promise and to wait and tarry until that blessing becomes ours personally.

Is Jesus coming again, and real soon? Will the aftermath of his coming (the rapture) be another terrible judgment time, the worst in history? Will history repeat itself? At his first coming, Jesus was largely rejected by his people. Are we, the church, making the same mistake? Who is on earth now to help each believer? Is He, too, being largely rejected? The Holy Ghost? Is He about to depart (the Restrainer)? What will be the result of that departure? Judgment!

That is why I watch, and look for opportunities to warn others. This is why the Lord might have given me that one word when I asked him what I could do next: MILLENNIALS. If they are not open to the gospel, the next thing for them will be a terrible wake-up call. Why? Because they, too, missed the time of their visitation. You have been warned. Are you now motivated to watch? Or will you, too, miss the time of your visitation? I pray, not! It does seem so many people are about to be blindsided, ambushed. Wake up before it is too late.

David F. Winecoff

Reader's Response to This Book:

1. Reader's name, age, and year born:

2. Why I read the book:

3. Present circumstances relating to working and parent's help:

4. Do you know younger people who are struggling? Will this book help them?

5. What is the primary problem with those educated in public schools (for example: codependent with a parent; laziness; no understanding of the real situation; poor schooling; bad choices; no gratitude, etc.) Do you personally know a young person who has failed to launch into life?

6. What impacted you personally in this book?

7. Authorization to use my name and response if this book is re-published, or a follow-up is written:

      YES   NO   (Circle one)

Signature:_____ Date:_____

Please email your response to: dwinecoff@fairpoint.net

One last thing: if you would like to view more of my thoughts and observations please visit my website at www.waragoodwarfare.com

A Challenge to Readers of This Book:

My intent in writing this book was to bless others. I asked God to help me write it so there would be an anointing on it. If you were so blessed, please consider taking a photo of the advertisement below with your smart phone and to help me spread the word. Share it with your email list, or on Facebook or Instagram.

If the message of this book impacted your life, give it a positive review on Amazon Books or any blog that you might regularly visit. Again, my purpose in writing this book was to bless others; not to profit from the Word of God. Thank you for considering this challenge.

----------********_____*********_____********_____

ABOUT THE AUTHOR

David F. Winecoff was born in a war zone in 1939 in Shanghai, China during the second year of his dad's three-year tour as a Lieutenant in the 4th Marine Regiment. Dave was raised on posts and stations around the Marine Corps and was commissioned a second lieutenant of Marines upon graduation from the University of Washington. He retired in 1983 after 21 years and three combat tours in Vietnam to begin speaking and writing about Spiritual Warfare. Dave posts writings at www.waragoodwarefare.com, and has self-published two books: "Forward March" and Secret Weapon." He has testified in many Christian Circles around the Pacific Northwest. Dave is the Chaplain of his local VFW Post. He and his wife have nine married children, 14 grandchildren and 15 great grandchildren. Both are active in Christian ministry.

Made in the USA
Middletown, DE
14 October 2021